PLAYING
DIRECTOR

14 DAY BOOK

**This book is due on or before
the latest date stamped below**

PLAYING DIRECTOR

A HANDBOOK FOR BEGINNERS

RICK DESROCHERS

HEINEMANN
PORTSMOUTH, NH

Heinemann
A division of Reed Elsevier Inc.
361 Hanover Street
Portsmouth, NH 03801-3912

Offices and agents throughout the world

We would like to thank those who have given their permission to include material
in this book. Every effort has been made to contact the copyright holders for
permission to reprint borrowed material where necessary. We regret any oversights
that may have occurred and would be happy to rectify them in future printings of
this work.

Excerpts from *The Dragon* by Paul Day. Copyright © 1991. Reprinted by permission of the author.

Library of Congress Cataloging-in-Publication Data
DesRochers, Rick.
    Playing director: a handbook for the beginning director/Rick DesRochers.
        p. cm.
    ISBN 0-435-08668-5 (alk. paper)
    1. Theater—Production and direction—Handbooks, manuals, etc.
I. Title.
PN2053.D48   1995
792' .0233—dc20
                                                                    95-4974
                                                                        CIP

Editor: Lisa A. Barnett
Cover illustration: Andrea Tamkin/The Fringe
Cover design: Catherine Hawkes

Printed in the United States of America on acid-free paper
98 97 96 95 DA 1 2 3 4 5 6

In memory of Daniel Witt and Bill Dobkin, great directors and friends both.

Thanks to director, teacher, and mentor Dick Trousdell for his support and inspiration, without which my career as a director (not to mention this book) would never have been possible.

And to Lisa Barnett, whose fine skill as an editor, and belief in this book, made it all happen.

"Faster, louder, funnier."
—Daniel Witt

Contents

Preface

So, You Have to Direct a Play?

T he process of directing a play involves not only how to go about it, but also why one does it in the first place. Even if you're asked by the school principal or the head of the English department to take on this responsibility, you must still come to terms with "why am I doing this," especially if you want to keep your sanity. As a teenager, I was constantly asking this question. "Why am I taking geometry?" "Why am I taking Introduction to Shakespeare?" "Will this get me anywhere?" "Is this important?" And especially, "How does this relate to me, and what I'll be doing after I graduate?" The best answer I could get was, "So that you can get into a good college." The worst answer I received was, "So you can graduate from high school." (Hmmm.) The school play was no exception in this regard. "Why should I do that!? I'll look like a geek and all my free time will be spent still at school! Rehearsing, of all things! And how am I going to convince my parents that this is important enough to spend so much time on?" These are the essential questions asked during high school. "What am I *after* by doing this?" "Why am I breaking my back to get this happening?" If you cannot answer these questions, then you are left with either rebellious or despondent students who either defy everything you say, or just don't give a damn. The same reasoning applies to acting and actors. Unless you can excite actors with your need and vision to do a play, they will either fight you every step of the way or be forced to work in a void without a cohesive and guiding vision. You do not have to be a brilliant artist of the theatre to do this. This is basic stuff, but without it your production will look half-hearted or chaotic. The quality of the school play reflects the climate and morale of a school just as much as the quality of a sports team does. So whether you are an experienced director or a beginner, these whys must be answered.

A teacher who is passionate about her subject always has the most exciting classes, no matter what the subject entails. I remember taking physics in high school, thinking it would be the most hateful class I had ever had—"No romance! No passion! No fun! No way in physics!"—yet the formula Mr. Grew permanently posted above the blackboard was P = F (Physics equals Fun). It was his passion about a subject that he loved that enabled me to enter the world of physics and to ace the class as well! The opposite was true in my early years of college when I took a course in Romantic poetry. I thought, "Wow! What passion! What romance! What fun!" No way. The instructor could have been reading from the phone book for all he seemed to care. The worst part was that I was an English major, and the thought that all my classes might be this boring was almost too much to handle. Luckily, a new Mr. Grew, in the form of Alberto Rios and creative writing, saved me with his vision and brought back my passion.

It is important that a teacher have a passion and drive for her subject, and the same can be said about directors. There is nothing more deadly than a director who brings no passion for the play or the actors to her work. "To do the play or not do the play" is not the only question. "Why am I doing this play or not doing this play," that is the question. "How can I bring passion, vision, and excitement to my students/actors and lead them to an entertaining and possibly fulfilling production of a play?" This is truly the question!

The living communication between live actors and audience, and the words of the playwright, creates a need for a theatre. Whether it is a professional, community, or student production, the commitment to a live (and lively) discussion of passions, ideas, and laughter is what is required to bring a play to life. Life and its myriad experiences are the shared stuff between actors and audience. For students, learning from life's experiences, working with fellow theatre artists, and sharing that experience with an audience makes any play worth producing. The production of a play is a journey that all take, ready to make discoveries and share adventures. This is what brings plays to life, and playwrights' words into the hearts and minds of actors, students, and audiences of all backgrounds. This is why we do the play. This is why we do theatre at all.

There is no one right way to direct a play. You may want to know, "Then, why am I reading this book?" Directors constantly find themselves challenged and pushed forward by the desire to create and find an answer to this elusive craft. So, how does one go about directing? How do you create this challenge? First of all, a director must get hired or at least be asked to direct. For some, directing can be an exciting challenge. The expectant director is thrilled and anticipates the experience with joy and embraces the challenge with eagerness. If the directing assignment was chosen for you, however, sometimes dread, fear, and hatred make the potential director balk at the new task. But no matter how you come to directing, you must be excited and motivated about the project. If you are not, the play is bound for disaster. The director is the energy and spirit behind any production, and the guiding force that creates the excitement and enthusiasm that the actors, designers, and technicians must have for a production to be successful. It is the director's energy, as well as the actors' and designers', that comes across the footlights. There is nothing more deadly to a production than an unenthusiastic director. The constant positive energy needed to get a production on its feet, from preproduction to rehearsal to opening night, is seemingly daunting but is necessary. The fate of all of the people working around you is in the director's hands.

Once you've decided to accept the challenge (with enthusiasm, of course), the real fun begins: picking the play. Usually, if you are hired, or even ordered, to direct a play, a certain project will be picked for you. "Well, Betsy, guess what? As head of the English department, you get to direct this year's production of *Our Town.*" Your eyes either light up or glaze over. Another typical scenario is having a "type" of project picked for you. "Hey, Frank, guess what? As the new teacher in history, we'd like for you to direct the school play. This year's theme is the history of the Native Americans." Is there such a play concerning the history of Native Americans? Where can you find something on the subject? Good questions. There are several play publishing and distributing companies in the United States (a partial listing can be found at the end of this book). You can call them for suggestions or request their catalogues. Or maybe you are asked to direct something more ambiguous. "Hey, Raoul, since you did plays in college, how about directing the school play? It has to be two one-act comedies." A likely response may be, "Oh, God, I don't even know *one* one-act comedy, never mind two!" Again, resources such as play publishers and bookstores can, and will, help.

If the choice is yours, however, how do you find something suitable for your actors, designers, and budget? First, find out what your budget and facilities are. If you have $100 and a classroom in which to work (you know, the old art room; just move the tables and benches around), this narrows your options. If you have $5,000 and the school auditorium, the possibilities open up. No matter how it comes about, your passion for the project must be of the utmost importance. You can always find creative ways around limitations of budgets and facilities, but never limit your imagination. It is your greatest resource. Never forget this. Creative solutions can be found to practical problems of staging, design, building of sets, and costumes, but no solutions are available for the uncommitted director. So, pick a project (if you have the choice) that excites you, and your actors/students will pick up on your enthusiasm and probably help you with solutions of their own. Passion is essential to any production, large or small. How can you get anyone excited about something in which *you* don't even believe? Unless you are a consummate actor and can give a constant and consistent performance, you are better off being genuinely passionate about the play at hand.

PLAYING

DIRECTOR

So, What Does a Director Do Anyway?

Here is a brief list defining the director's role. A director is a

mother
father
teacher (of history, art, sociology)
mentor
manager
carpenter
electrician
"fix-it" person
psychologist
advisor
salesperson
friend
protector
person with a vision to share

Now are you intimidated? This simple list is helpful for beginning to understand what a director is and does. Please don't be discouraged. Why? Because being multifaceted is what makes directing exciting and fulfilling, no matter what that person's experience. Let's say your principal calls you and says, "Next year, you will be teaching English 1 and Creative Writing 2, and you will be assigned cafeteria duty, must chair PTA meetings, and direct the school play." Your reaction is, "What? I'm sorry? What? Direct the what?" The principal answers, "The school play. The pride and image of the entire school is on the line, and you've got to come through for the school's sake." Your response is, "Oh." Now what? Go back to the list. You may think you need all of these people to help you (and you do), but you need to be all of them put together, and it's not impossible. You need to embrace all of these qualities within yourself, and go for it! I am not being facetious. This need is real and it is possible, but you have to make it happen. Remember, a school theatre club and a professional theatre are both dependent on the quality of their productions, and the director is the key figure in bringing out the qualities of the actors/students and the institution itself.

The Evolution of the Director

The role of the director is a relatively recent one. One of the first self-proclaimed directors was George II, the Duke of Saxe-Meiningen, who worked as such during the late 1800s. Before this, the role of director came in the person of the actor-manager, a person such as Molière or Shakespeare, who not only wrote plays but also acted in and produced them as well. The purpose of the director was not the same as we know it today, but it was still in evidence. The idea of a play coordinator was unnecessary because plays were performed without our contemporary technical sense of design in costumes, lights, and sets. In fact, Molière's and Shakespeare's theatres used available lighting, either daylight or candlelight, and, with the exception of special costume pieces, such as the ass's head in *A Midsummer Night's Dream*, used clothing of the period. In this era, the theatre space itself was used as the setting. "Production values" did not exist. The theatre of Molière and Shakespeare was focused solely on the actor and the plays. The actors' roles were even created to reflect the abilities and personalities of specific actors in the companies. Staging, or blocking, consisted of getting people on and off of the stage as efficiently as possible. Molière's texts were broken down into scenes according to the entrances and exits of the characters.

It was not until the advent of such stage designers/directors as Gordon Craig and Adolphe Appia that the entire production became coordinated, choreographed, and designed—and the role of the director emerged. These various elements needed to be managed and translated to the actors and production team to create a cohesive whole. As a side note, the advent of Alfred Jarry's *Ubu Roi* in 1886 paved the way for modern theatre production. Until this time, Western theatre was concentrated on recognizable types of people—the courtier, the clown, kings and queens—but with Jarry's play came an unrealistic theatrical world never before witnessed by audiences. No longer were there recognizable locations of the court or its surrounding forests. Instead there emerged a place, a time, and characters that had no realistic or historical basis. Basing his play on satire and larger-than-life characters, Jarry created a new theatre language that took plays away from the everyday world and placed them in an entirely new context. But what was this context to be? How should it be staged and designed? (It should be noted that certain plays, such as Shakespeare's *A Midsummer Night's Dream*, also contain elements of unknown worlds, and many non-Western theatre traditions are based on mythological and spiritual worlds.) Not only were the elements of subsequent design and staging affected by this shift in worldview, but also the acting technique itself shifted from formal and traditional forms of entertainment to one that demanded an outside, objective eye to create it. A new vision of the play was needed that would come from outside the actual production and could coordinate all of these new elements.

At about this same time, the theatre was undergoing another major transformation because of playwrights such as Strindberg, Ibsen, and Chekhov, who created characters based on psychological observations that required a new study of acting and characterizations. The Moscow Art Theatre, under the leadership of Stanislavski (also an actor), was looking at an entirely new, more naturalistic approach to acting to accommodate these plays. Meyerhold, also from the Moscow Art Theatre, was experimenting with a staging and acting style called biomechanics, which had its roots in gymnastics, the circus, and the music hall. No longer was the theatre dedicated to the elegant presentation of characters who would stride forth to centerstage and deliver set speeches. Now, staging, acting, and designs of plays reflected "the world" in which they took place. The audience was taken into an unfamiliar world, and for this to happen, the production required a form that could interpret these elements and create a world full of detail and mystery—a world of wonders. This was a world that could be created only in the theatre.

The Theatre as Magic

To understand plays and their staging, we must realize that they are derived from the theatrical tradition. They are not fully realized texts, as are novels or stories, which are complete in and of themselves. They are skeletons which we flesh out with the ideas and actions of actors, designers, and all of the theatre artists who contribute to the production of the play. There is no "right way" to produce a play. The theatre has its own set of rules and conventions which give it a life separate from television and film. The theatre has its own magic. By this I mean that anything is possible once a stage convention has been established. There is a certain stage language that exists. A simple example of this can be found in a production of Shakespeare's *Pericles* that I saw (directed by Mark Lamos at The Hartford Stage Company), in which an actor was "drowning" in the ocean. To create this moment, a sheet of plastic was thrown over the actor, who was lying on the stage floor, and as he struggled with the plastic over him, he created the illusion of drowning and being caught up in the waves of the ocean. No elaborate, realistic staging was necessary; only a simple idea that created a moving and theatrical moment. The audience does not need a literal action on stage to help them understand the action of the play. Like a magician, the actor can create or transform objects and her own body from one thing, place, or person to another, without a literal shifting of person, place, or thing. The actor makes it "appear" for the audience by engaging the audience's imagination. This is where the work of the director with the actors becomes all-important. The director brings these theatrical forms to life by creating stage metaphors and conventions which the audience is asked to accept as the "reality" of the play's world. It is the creation of this stage framework that makes the director's job, and the theatre itself, distinct from modern technological forms such as television, film, and video.

The Responsibilities of the Director

Theatre is a collaboration of artists and technicians. It is the director's job to coordinate all of these personalities and combine them into one vision for the play's production. Usually out of necessity, it is often the director who must take on the tasks of designer, stage manager, electrician, set builder, and house manager. Theatre takes a dedication that most students and even some professionals cannot give. The director, therefore, must have that dedication and be ready to cover all bases at all times. As a director, I've taken up slack in all of these areas and sometimes learned as I went along. To avoid unnecessary surprises, create a list of personnel, such as the one that follows, that you need to produce your show. Realize that if you don't have this staff, you may have to do these jobs yourself.

Production Staff
production manager
stage manager
publicity coordinator
house manager

Technicians and Crew
master electrician
technical director
set builder
costume builder
light and sound board operators
costume and set crews

Artistic Staff
director
designers (set, costume, lights, props, sound)
actors

All of these positions are necessary for a production, but many can be doubled as duties overlap and volunteers become scarce. Once you've got the necessary list, your responsibility is to recruit individuals for these jobs. (Additional information on recruiting and creating an effective staff is found in subsequent chapters.)

Remember that it is the essential coordination and constant nurturing of these various individuals that become the director's focus. A large part of the director's job is to create excitement and nurture the talents and ideas of individuals. This is the director's reward, as well as the ultimate accomplishment: the building of a creative team that can work together and create an innovative and provocative production of which all members of the team can be proud.

So, Where Do Plays Come from Anyway? Or, There Is No Santa Claus 2

Picking a Play Suitable for Your Actors (and Your Budget)

The play should be picked always with the students/actors in mind. What are their needs? What are their age groups and backgrounds? What are their day-to-day problems and frustrations? Even if you wish to produce a frivolous and light-hearted production, you still have to take these things into account. There are many kinds of comedies or mysteries from which to choose. For example, Noel Coward wrote comedies, but hardly the kind that high school or even college students would be able to undertake, or even want to perform. The plays of Alan Ayckbourn and Neil Simon have an adult sophistication and social background that could confuse and alienate your cast. So, start by evaluating the students and their needs. Once you determine this, then you have narrowed down the task of deciding which play to produce. There are several play publishing companies, all of whom have annual catalogues to help you discover plays that you had no idea even existed. There are a few companies, such as Baker's Plays and Dramatic Play Publishing, that specialize in plays for children and young adults. Read the descriptions and order single copies of plays that interest you, and then read them. You will know right away whether these plays are suitable for your students and your budget.

Once you've found the play you like, sit down with it and read it, and enjoy yourself. Try to picture yourself as an audience member. Where do you laugh, cry, and get angry? These signposts in an early reading will determine where you place emphasis in rehearsal and, consequently, in performance. Your first instincts about staging, designs, and so forth, are usually very important to what you would like to see happen in the play. (What would interest me? How did I respond to that scene?) You are not under the pressures of technical deadlines and rehearsals during which actors ask millions of questions, so take this time to dream and enjoy the play and its many facets. If you don't, you will not get to know the play well enough to be confident in directing it, and your choices will not be clear when you are in the midst of rehearsals. You must have a clear idea of what you want to see in each and every scene of the play on stage. Although this may change as you work with actors and designers, your vision of the play remains instrumental in keeping the course of the play consistent and relevant. Always remember why you chose the play and how it made you feel. These instincts will inform all of your choices and decisions later on. As the production progresses, you can always refer back to the initial reading and your notes as a place from which to hang your choices. If this play stimulates your imagination, then it is the one for you.

Okay, So You've Picked a Play—Now What?

Anything that is created and copyrighted or patented becomes the property of the originator. The originator of the materials in question receives monies for her invention/writing. Royalties are the way a playwright makes her living. Just as a computer software developer or novelist receives compensation for her work, so does the playwright. When a school, company, or individual decides to produce a play that has a copyright and has been published, you must compensate the writer for the use of her work. After all, it is her work, and the play would not exist nor be known to you without her efforts. Plays do not fall from the sky; they are written by human beings who have to make a living just like you, so you must be respectful of the fact that royalties keep the playwright alive and writing.

Royalties are monies paid to the author of a play for using her work. Play publishers act as the author's agent. They collect the monies and create the contracts for the rights to produce plays. Sometimes there are restrictions and certain plays are not available for production at the time you wish to produce the play. The restrictions of plays occur when a play is, due to wishes of the author and agent, not available for production. For example, if another production of a play is being produced at the same time that you plan to do yours, you may not be able to do the play, thereby thwarting potential competition between the two productions. Or if a national tour of a play is currently being produced, you may be restricted from producing the play. The production rights for these productions have been given exclusively to one theatre company by the author's agent, and you must wait until those rights have been released. At other times, playwrights may wish to rewrite or have a revival of a play, and will want time to rewrite or work on the play before it is made available for general production. It is ultimately up to the playwright and agent to decide what restrictions apply. It is therefore important that you contact the publishing company or agent as soon as you know which play you want to direct. You can get verbal confirmation that a play is available, but you must get the contract in writing before it is considered legal to proceed with a production.

Getting the rights to produce a play is fairly simple. Again, the play publishing companies can give you this information. (There is a list of play publishers at the end of this book.) It is important to obtain the rights to a play in writing well in advance of the production. Not obtaining production rights is unprofessional and can get you into trouble, not only with the publisher and author, but also with your school board. It creates a bad reputation for you and your school/company and makes the chances of getting the rights for other productions difficult. Don't risk it. Get the rights.

So, You Have to Prepare a Play? 3

reparation is one of the most important aspects of directing. Coupled with the rehearsal work, preparation is essential to the directing of a play. The following is a list of steps that was developed from a directing class I taught at the New Theatre, Inc., in Boston. My students had been frustrated, and rightfully so, by the lack of rules or guidelines that could be applied to the director's craft. Although I had never before put a director's way of thinking into concrete terms, their request did not seem unreasonable to me. In fact, I accepted it as a challenge to come up with some way of making the process of directing less ephemeral and more practical. I had to analyze my own process of directing, and by doing so, discovered that there were certain aspects of preparation and rehearsal techniques that I employed. Listed are twenty-eight steps for a director to follow. They should be taken with a grain of salt, and are certainly not intended as a definitive answer to all of the questions of the directing world, but are intended as a guideline for making the process of directing a show a little less daunting.

1. *Find a text.* (This also is covered in Chapter 2.)
   The emphasis here again is on finding a text that is appropriate for the group of actors, designers, and staff

with whom you are working, and any school or community-related projects, classes, or events.

2. *Read it for fun.*
   When you read a play for the first time, it should be for your own pleasure. Put yourself in the audience and see the play as an audience member would. Try not to worry about how you're going to do the play, but let yourself be entertained. Let your imagination go and just enjoy the words, ideas, and emotions from a purely objective point of view.

3. *Read it for meaning* (intellectual understanding).
   Now that you've had your fun, go back and read the play for its overt meaning. What is this play talking about? Do you understand all the words, the jargon, what the characters are trying to say? Look in any historical, literary, or technical source for information that you don't understand. Sometimes a character is referring to a specific region, ethnic group, or historical event that can color the way a text is read. Don't get caught assuming anything. Actors will be looking to you for both intellectual and emotional information, and you must be ready to at least help them in their understanding of the text. That's your job.

4. *Read it for emotional responses.*
   This one is a purely subjective reading. How does this play make you feel? Don't go overboard. Is the overall tone fun, melancholic, chaotic, logical, frightening, ethereal? Where do you laugh or cry or get angry or have fun? These initial responses will usually end up in the final product. Your emotional reaction will inform the way you direct the entire play and will enhance specific scenes. You have to trust that your responses are genuine and valid. You are the director, and it is your guidance of the play, emotionally as well as intellectually, that creates the rehearsal atmosphere, which will be transferred by the actors to the performances.

5. *Read it for sensory responses.*
   Every play involves the five senses. These are your most valuable tools. Like a musician's feeling for music, you can understand a play without using your intellect. Close your eyes and imagine the images, sounds, colors, textures, and scents as each scene unfolds. Read a scene and make note of any sensory responses you encounter. (This is covered in more detail later in this chapter.)

(Steps 3, 4, and 5 will happen either separately, together, or in a different order.)

6. *Read it aloud to yourself.*
   Get a feeling for the rhythm of the text; that is, how it will be spoken by the actors and heard by the audience. Like poetry, a play has a distinct rhythm that builds with the action of the play. Think of yourself as a conductor hearing the various characters' voices and sounds of movement. Again, close your eyes and be a spectator trying to hear the play as an audience member would.

7. *Get a sense of the whole picture before you start to think in specifics.*
   Through all of the steps given so far, you have been creating an overall impression of the play: creating internal responses for yourself that are creating the world of the play. The details of staging and rehearsal of specific scenes and moments will become much easier if you have done this preliminary work and have a sense of the whole picture. You will not get caught up later in details that will bog you down, nor have to worry about how you are going to stage a particular part. Trust your instincts and let yourself respond to the play on a gut level.

8. *Take a shower and relax.*
   Take a break. Live your life.

9. *Go to work.*

10. *Read the text again.*
    Get a feel for how the story unfolds. Plays are about storytelling. The audience has to be "going somewhere." You're taking them on a journey into the world of your play. Try to follow the story as an audience member would.

11. *Answer the question, "What is the journey?"*
    A better question might be, "What is *a* journey?" A journey involves the audience's imagination. A play is a new world for the audience. You are taking them into this world through the journey. A play follows a storyline. You're telling the story through the *action* of the play. What is happening on stage? What is happening to the characters? What literally happens scene by scene to advance the storyline? Plays are about actions. As each action unfolds, the story advances and takes the audience along with it.

    • Whose journey is it?
    • Whose perspective determines the journey? (Which character or characters tell the story?)

12. *Decide how other characters reflect or interact with, and off of, the main character or characters, as defined in step 11.*

13. *Take another shower.*

14. *Go to work.*

15. *Synthesize the major theme or journey of the text into a single sentence (statement) or even a single phrase or word.*
    By distilling the vision of the play into a single phrase or sentence, the director can keep the direction of the play more focused. Every choice must respond to this statement. For example, in Paul Day's *The Dragon*, one possibility is the phrase "creating your own fears." Our leading character, Cass, creates her worst fear by letting her anger make her into what she hates most, the dragon that she thinks killed her mother. Now in some way, shape, or form, all of the characters create their own fears. Cass's father, Giacomo, also creates his own fear of losing his daughter by pushing her away emotionally because of his grief over his wife's death. Cass leaves home because she feels unwanted. Her anger and loss make her seek out the dragon, and the cycle of becoming what you fear continues. Thus, one action leads to another, and all stem from the director's initial statement. You can now trace the actions of the other characters and see how this affects the entire journey of the play. Other examples of a play with its corresponding focus-statement are *King Lear*, "sight from blindness"; and *Ubu Roi*, "a fenced-in playground."

16. *Picture the entire show as would an audience member.*
    - Hear it.
    - See it.
    - Laugh with it.
    - Cry with it.
    - Get angry with it.
    - Have fun with it!

    In other words, cast yourself as an audience member. You *are* the audience during the rehearsal process.

17. *Put down the text and your notes for a few days, and do not think about the play at all.*
    Allow your ideas to settle inside of you.

18. *Now go back to the text and see if your impressions still remain the same.*
    If your impressions have changed, don't be afraid to rethink and refeel them, but remember that your first impressions are often the ones you should trust, because they come from the unconscious and are uncensored.

19. *Begin discussions with designers and production team.*
    See Chapter 8.

20. *Cast the play.*
    See Chapter 5.

21. *Rehearse, and try out your ideas with the actors.*
    This is the real work and a trial ground for testing your previously discovered instincts and understanding of the play.

22. *Technical rehearsals.*
    See Chapters 4 and 8.

23. *Hold the final dress rehearsal.*
    See Chapters 8 and 9.

24. *Take a shower.*

25. *Go to work.*

26. *Enjoy opening night* (or "the heart attack," not to mention the relief).
    The work now has a life of its own. Enjoy it.

27. *Say "goodbye" to the show.*
    You, the cast, and the crew, through your play, have become great friends. You have lived with these people and characters for weeks, and suddenly they are gone. The show is over. Spending such a short and intensely intimate time with a project that involves other people and their emotions can create a scenario that is difficult to leave behind. Make sure that you prepare your cast and yourself for this possibility. The experience lives in the moment that it is happening; it is therefore ephemeral. Having an understanding of this will make saying goodbye to the experience a little easier.

28. *Repeat steps 1 through 27.*

Researching the Play

All plays require research. A play takes place in a specific environment, whether it be sixteenth-century Elizabethan England or 1990's New England. Even mythical environments, such as the long-ago small village in Paul Day's *The Dragon* or the fairy forest in *A Midsummer Night's Dream*, can be based in a recognizable atmosphere. This is "the world of the play." In fact, you are creating a new world that is unique to each play every time it is produced. Research can help you ground your choices for this theatrical world. When working with designers and actors, your research can give you a visual and intellectual support to guide your ideas. The production team has to be wooed into believing in your vision of the play. Research gives you the background necessary to give your vision a firm footing. In *Miss Jairus*, by Michel de Ghelderode, which takes place in sixteenth-century Belgium, I found historical information from that era through histories and biographies, but most of my research revolved around the artwork of Breughel the Elder, who painted people and scenes from the period. Through research on the playwright, I discovered that Ghelderode was greatly influenced by Breughel and actually wrote plays based on his paintings.

Researching the Playwright

Although playwrights and their plays are not necessarily interwoven, researching their histories and reading their other plays (and any other published works about them), you can begin to understand how certain aspects of each play are influenced by their personal experiences. Again, in the case of Ghelderode, I knew that his influences as a theatrical writer came from the 1920's music hall and marionette shows. This experience figured into the stylization of his play. With newer playwrights who do not yet have a significant body of work, this task can be harder; but usually one can find interviews or articles on the playwrights or their plays, or even reviews of their productions. If the playwrights are still living, you have one great advantage in that you can actually contact them and possibly talk with them. A director-friend of mine was working on Michel Tremblay's *Albertine in Five Times* and actually traveled to Canada to meet and talk with Tremblay. She got a real sense of the playwright—how he spoke, what his interests were—and also saw him in the environment that influenced his work. They discussed her uncertainties and confirmed other ideas. This interaction stimulated a lot of decisions that she subsequently made in the production. Again, it is not necessary to do exactly what the playwright had in mind. Each production will have its own identity by virtue of the fact that it involves different theatre artists, whose work will differ greatly from production to production. It can never hurt, however, to get all of the information available and then make your decisions accordingly, even though they may be radically different from the author's original intentions. It is up to a director to pick and choose what works for her and her vision of a play, and how it will influence the production.

The worst director is one who is unprepared. A director who goes to rehearsals without proper knowledge of the play will soon be found out. Doing your homework is all-important. The actors and staff are looking to you for guidance. You wouldn't show up to a construction sight without blueprints from which to work. Imagine an architect telling a contractor, "Well, we'll sorta start over here, and put that over there, maybe." Hardly. In this same manner, the director must show up with blueprints as well. Although you can try different ways of creating theatrical moments throughout the rehearsal process, you will be able to change with the needs of the moment by doing your homework and having a full grasp of the play.

The Blueprints

All plays need *theatrical* blueprints before you can begin preproduction planning and rehearsals. You create a plan that others can follow. You also create a language (perhaps for the first time) that everyone will use in the weeks that follow. It is imperative that the director communicate with the production team and the actors. Because each play is a completely new experience for everyone involved, it is necessary that the director create an approach to the work that provides a basis for communication. There are no two ways about it—directing is about being a good communicator. Your job is to inform actors, designers, and technical assistants about what you want and how they are to achieve it. You also must get all of these people to work effectively *with each other.* Just as scientists, doctors, plumbers, mechanics, and other professionals have a vocabulary, both visual and verbal, that has been created to deal with the job at hand, so do theatre professionals. You need to know not only the technical vocabulary of the theatre, but also how it *applies* to the play. I have compiled seven basic terms and concepts that you will need to communicate with your staff: action, time, place, movement, rhythm, paintings, music, and space. As you read the play over and over again, consider these elements. They will affect the way you work with other creative artists and give you a way to create an effective dialogue with them.

ACTION

The core of any play, act, scene, or monologue is action. What's happening?—not what is being said, but what is actually going on physically and emotionally in the moment. In order for actors to understand character, they must discover what the character does.

What they say is obvious. It's written for all to see. What they do while they are speaking is how the characters come alive. As Teach says in *American Buffalo*, "Action walks and bullshit talks." And so it is with people. It is action that tells the story of who a person is. A scene from *Waiting for Godot* illustrates this perfectly. Gogo says to Didi, "Let's go," but they do not move. If we take these words literally, the characters would indeed go, and the entire point of the play would be lost. This simple choice of action (that is, *not* to go) describes the fear and frustration of the characters better than any monologue about the subject.

Actors can relate far more readily to actions (doing something) than to abstract thoughts such as, "Oh, the character feels like this, or he's *that* kind of person." Body language, movement, and how a character "acts" is the key to character and the actual staging of the play.

As a director, you must ask yourself some basic questions about the action of the play. What actually happens during the play? What overall action or actions take place? For example, in a murder mystery, the overall action is the discovery of the murderer. The murder and the actual investigation are actions that lead up to the climactic action of the discovery. How do the characters interact? Do they *say* what they actually do? You need to break down each scene in terms of action. Sometimes it is helpful to give each scene a title in terms of the action. The scene in *Godot*, given earlier, could be stated as, "They make to leave, but do not move." This explains what the characters are *doing* in the scene (that is, not moving) as opposed to what is being talked about.

TIME

When does the play take place? Does it reflect an historical period? A contemporary one? If the play takes place in the present or "now," when was it written? Is the action of the play continuous? Is it broken up at all? For example, does the play take place over the course of a day, a week, or a year, or does it move back and forth in time? Are there flashbacks to other time periods? The timeframe also will locate the place of the play. Thirteenth-century Scotland is a far cry from twentieth-century Scotland.

PLACE

Where does the action literally take place? Is it inside, outside, on a farm, in the street, in South Africa, in Tokyo, or in a mythological kingdom? Do the settings change at all? Do they move from one locale to another? Do they move from one time period to another?

MOVEMENT/RHYTHM

How does the play move? Are the scenes short or long, or do they vary in length? How are they connected by the action? Does the play have a high energy or a more somber tone? How does this effect the way the characters move and speak on stage? How is dramatic tension built by the way the characters interact with each other and their environment? Rhythm is created out of the relationship between the overall movement of the play and how the characters create that movement through their actions. (See also the later section on music.)

PAINTINGS

All plays have images that are found in their language and stories. A play is a visual, as well as an aural, experience. Having a certain painting or artist's work in mind will give you a framework from which to work visually. From paintings, and other fine artwork, you can understand what colors, textures, and compositions can be used in your play. Plays are about movement in a three-dimensional space, and about how the characters interact in that space. To understand spatial and character relationships better and to determine, with designers, what would be the best visual choices, you must be able to see the play in its context of color and movement. Paintings give you ideas about staging and give the entire production team a place to start forming their ideas about design.

MUSIC

Now that you've determined the time and action of the play, what kind of music does the play evoke within you? This can determine the pacing and overall rhythm of the play and can give you insight into how the various scenes interrelate. When actors speak, a certain rhythm and pacing is created. To give this sound shape, having an idea of what kind of music your play sounds like can help shape the play aurally. This is purely subjective to the director and is one of the aesthetic choices that a director makes. Close your eyes. Does the play sound like a Bach concerto or a Jimi Hendrix solo? Like the text of a musical score, your play follows certain patterns, chords, and time signatures. Unlike a musical score, however, a play is only a skeleton from which you improvise. So, a play would be more like jazz, in that a certain pattern of chords and timing is involved, but your actors and designers can improvise from the basic chords (the script), making the play and its experience unique.

SPACE

Thinking about spatial relationships in plays is much like design-ing an effective way of organizing a room in a house. Your must think of the room and its relationship to the rest of the house. Be-cause most people are not lucky enough to design and have their houses built for them, you must work with the existing house with its existing rooms. The relationship between the characters and their environment creates the "space" of the play. Two lone actors on a tiny, bare stage create a theatrical statement of isolation and intimacy, just as a chorus of costumed dancers kick-lining in front of a colorful backdrop creates an environment of expansive high energy and mass excitement.

When you think of space, you must think of the stage and its relationship to the environment of the theatre. How does the audi-ence member perceive the play in the context of the theatre's ar-chitecture? Because this is not film or television, people and objects are in a live, three-dimensional relationship to the audi-ence. The distances and sizes of the actual stage and auditorium must therefore be taken into consideration. Does the space of the play need to be large and expansive or tight, closed, and claustro-phobic? Do you need a large stage or a smaller one to accommo-date the action, scenery, and characters? Is there a way of creating the illusion of a larger or smaller space by altering the audience's perspective of the stage and its spatial relationship to the charac-ters? Putting characters in the audience creates a sense of space that is quite different from confining them to the stage. Creating a wide gap between the audience and the front of the stage creates a sense of disconnected distance between audience and performer. The question of space needs attention because it affects your choices in design, blocking, and character relationships.

Creating the World of the Play

THROUGH IMAGES, SOUNDS, AND SEEING THE PLAY IN YOUR MIND'S EYE

When you first read a play, how do you feel? Do you respond on a personal level? I remember that the first time I read *Curse of the Starving Class*, I was so moved that I immediately reread it. It spoke to me. What made it come to life was not only the story of a family being torn apart, but also its atmosphere, its gut-punch language, and its vivid characterizations. If you can see a play come to life in your imagination, you can begin to direct the play. Think of the play as action. What is happening to the people as they speak? Where are they standing? How are they standing? Is anyone moving? Are there any sounds or music? What are the people who are *not* speaking doing? Your job is to create the world of the play.

The use of visual and aural stimuli can be a great starting point when creating your own theatrical world. All of these influences come from your individual response to the play's text. What images and sounds does the playwright choose to describe? Relating these ideas to other artistic references will create a rich and textural world of sights, sounds, and theatrical entertainment. Create a simple list of images, nouns, verbs, sounds, and colors that are mentioned or inferred in the script. Remember that the text is the key to finding these responses. Always use the text as your point of reference.

Two ways of seeing and hearing the world of the play—through paintings and music/sound—have been discussed earlier, but merit further attention in this present context.

Through Paintings ■ One of my greatest references for designers and actors alike is taken from paintings. Artwork creates a world where characters live and a space for them to be living *in*. One of the world's greatest mysteries (dramas) is the smile of the *Mona Lisa*. Think of the different stories that people have devised to explain that smile and that woman. The important thing is not to find the correct answer to the question of why, but to find what you *see* when you look at the painting. What world is being evoked for you? Don't try to figure it out, just respond.

When directing *Miss Jairus*, I grounded the visual and emotional aspects of the play in Breughel's sixteenth-century painting, *The Kermess* (The Peasant Dance). This painting gave me not only an historical locale, but also a sense of color, movement, and spatial relationships that transferred into the acting, blocking, and design of the play. If you can convey to your cast and designers that this is the world in which you see the play, they can respond to the artwork and have a starting point from which to create. Then, everyone has a reference point. Not only did the painting give visual ideas, but also gave an historical context from which to work. We began researching the time period of the painting and its social implications, and this informed the background and character choices for the actors. I remember that the most important aspect of the Breughel was the color and movement of the painting. Those colors were transformed into the lighting and costumes of the play, and the movement pattern of a chaotic, superstitious, carnival-like atmosphere informed the movement patterns and stage setting. The atmosphere of the fairground became the central metaphor for the entire production—a carnival where everything is permitted and no rules apply to the behavior of the people. The characters wore masks to give the expression of hard-worn peasant faces that were exaggerated, as in the world of the painting. The only time the peasants of this time period could be themselves and let themselves go wild was during the harvest dances. Once this was established, my job became one of how to create the atmosphere of this sixteenth-century world based on the research of the period and the visual images that the painting evoked. All of my choices revolved around this visual reference, but I did not attempt to copy it. I only created impressions of it found through my own responses.

Through Music/Sound ■ Music creates an emotional atmosphere that informs the rhythm and emotional world of the play. Sound is very subjective. Different forms of music can create many different responses within people. In *Miss Jairus*, I heard the sounds and music of the fairgrounds. The cacophony of the carnival with its mad calliope, the noises of the crowds, and sounds of games, bells, and dogs barking, all served to create the aural world of the play. When actors made their entrances, it was with the energy and intensity of children rushing into the fairgrounds, running from one game to the next. Everything was bright lights and colors. The carnival barker's "Hurry, hurry, step right up!" and the chance to the see the mysterious and the unknown created an exhilarating and frightening world of sound.

Character Analysis

Each character should be drawn vividly in the director's mind—not necessarily the physical "type" but the emotional and psychological qualities of each individual. Every character makes a journey throughout the course of the play. Every character wants something and goes on this journey to get it. Some succeed and some do not, but all try to achieve their goals. This gives the play its dramatic life. It is this journey you are discovering with the actors. Again, research can help. Any available background about the people and their environment, customs, and social/economic status can help the actors better understand the characters and create more vivid portrayals.

Special Production Needs

Another aspect of research is understanding any special skills or environments on which the play focuses. For example, Caryl Churchill's play *Serious Money* creates the life and environment of the big-city stockmarket right after the Big Bang. The language, movement, and actions depend on a clear understanding of the world of the stockmarket. Any information you can get by visiting a broker or seeing the floor of the stock exchange in action can help. When directing David Mamet's *American Buffalo*, the scene designer and I traveled to various pawn shops to understand the architecture as well as the environment in which the play took place. Because we knew that pawn shops were found mostly in large cities, we went to Boston and New York and entered these shops as potential customers to have a real dialogue and experience of the places. Plays that take place in different regions and environments have to be researched for the differences in lifestyle and cultural values.

Special subject matter, such as medical conditions, must be researched. Topics such as AIDS, suicide, and teen pregnancy are subjects that may affect characters directly or indirectly. If a play takes place in a hospital or clinic, going to these places and talking to people, employees, and clientele will make your production richer and more textured. If you have not done your homework, you may insult your audience. For example, I'm sure that everyone has seen a production in which a character must appear to be intoxicated or even alcoholic, and the actor staggers around the stage "acting" drunk. Playing stereotypes like this can be insulting and makes your production look ridiculous and empty. It can never hurt to get as much authentic information as possible. Libraries are an obvious place for research, but life experiences are always more valuable. If an actor does not have the life experience necessary to play the character credibly, she must do some personal research to fill in the gaps of her actual experience.

Film and video are good research tools for exploring locations you cannot afford to actually go and see. Films that take place in foreign countries can give you an idea of cultural customs and dialects and can give actors a sense of the environment. There are many other options for research, examples of which are discussed in the following sections.

MUSEUMS

Museums are great places for delving into the cultural aspects of foreign communities that you cannot afford to visit in person.

SPECIAL EXHIBITS

I have often gone to special exhibits to conduct research. I once attended a boat show because the play demanded a thorough knowledge of boats and their histories. Using this research option, you not only get to see a particular exhibit, but also can talk to people who are very knowledgeable about specific subjects. These talks with people usually are the most valuable information you can get, next to actual experience.

CONCERTS

Concerts will provide firsthand exposure to musical styles. Just as in the theatre, a true *musical* experience only happens with live music. You may even get a chance to speak with musicians about the various nuances of their music.

MAPS

Maps are a great source of information for understanding the borders and terrain of particular regions. In some parts of the world, these borders are constantly shifting, and the struggle over land is an all-important and lifelong issue. Also, the terrain of the country can affect the atmosphere and mood particular to a play. For example, Ibsen certainly is influenced by the Fjords of Norway—both his characters and stage environments are deeply affected by this geographical construct.

BOOKS

Both fiction and nonfiction can be good sources of background information on cultures and regional qualities. William Faulkner and Toni Morrison write about the American South, but in completely different ways and from completely different points of view. Comparing and contrasting these different viewpoints can often lead to dispelling certain stereotypes and helping you to rethink things often taken for granted as being "true" about a particular region.

MAGAZINES

Magazines are a great source of contemporary visual information. If you cannot attend specific exhibits or shows, magazines can give you information on particular subjects. There must be a specialty magazine for just about every profession and hobby on the planet.

These elements of research are essential for visualizing and shaping your play. You must have a strong impression of the play before you begin production meetings and rehearsals. You are guiding a group of creative artists, and it is up to you to be able to communicate effectively with them so they can do their work in collaboration with the other artists involved.

So, What Are the Technical Considerations? 4

I f you are on a limited budget and have a limited staff, keep it simple! Don't overburden yourself. Some of the most effective theatre comes from simplicity. Elabo rate sets, costumes, and lighting have their place, and a big spectacle can be exciting and fun, but let's face it, the theatre is about human beings and their relationships. Without this human underpinning, a play is meaningless. If we look at theatre from the time of ancient Greece and follow it to the present day, a simple list of the work of playwrights will confirm that plays concern themselves with human relationships first and foremost. Euripides, Shakespeare, Chekhov, Molière, Beckett, and even more abstract playwrights such as Pinter and Ionesco, based their themes in humankind's search for meaning and understanding within this complex universe. All plays focus on this basic quest. What is humankind's relationship to other human beings and the surrounding universe? Even the simplest of murder mysteries explores the psychology of the murderer and the suspects' interpersonal relationships. You cannot escape this fact.

Waiting for Godot, one of the world's most analyzed plays (go to the library and see for yourself!), has a basic and simple theme—two men trying to discover exactly what it is they are waiting around for! Why are they here? Their constant quest for an answer to this question creates the conflict and drama of the play. I discovered another example of simplicity when I witnessed a very beautiful production of a play called *Poppie Nongena*. In this production, a South African acting company (six members) recreated an entire township and its struggle against apartheid. In order to focus on the play's characters, the production was stripped of all "flashy" staging. A basic piece of corrugated tin was used to represent everything from a simple shelter to a musical instrument. The tin was representative of the corrugated tin shelters that the Blacks of South Africa are forced to use for housing. This material was always present and, by virtue of being unobtrusive, helped to focus the action of the play on the characters, but remained a constant reminder of the poverty and humiliation of the characters. It allowed the action to flow freely from shelters to a jail cell to the street without scene changes, which would have distracted from the human relationships of the play.

There is nothing worse than watching stage hands moving in dim lights, changing the scenery and disrupting the action, during a blackout. There is absolutely no reason for this, unless you are trying to create moments of interrupted action in the play's structure. In *Poppie Nongena*, the use of the corrugated tin created a representative change in time and place without having to create a literal change in scenery and environment (therefore interrupting the action) and gave the director (and actors) more time to focus on the characters of the play and less time on resetting the scenery and changing costumes. This sounds simple enough, but believe me, it is ultimately very important to the entire action of the play.

Imagination

Imagination is your most valuable asset. When looking at a play with a realistic set that takes place in a room with four walls, it is not necessary to build walls with working doors and windows, even if you can afford it. Usually, the building of box sets (a set with realistic walls) will result in flimsy, often dangerous scenery that usually ends up falling down rather than staying upright. In depicting the set of a medieval courtyard in *Miss Jairus*, the scene designer decided that a textured flooring (created with spattered paint) and a simple freestanding door conveyed the effect quite well, and it was the actors' relationship to their environment that created the feeling of the courtyard. Once you establish the space according to consistent blocking and groundplan, your audience members can supply the walls and windows in their imaginations. The great advantage of theatre over film and TV is that the audience can accept nonrealistic and representational ideas. We do not need to give the audience everything. This is the excitement and power of live theatre. Like a magic act, it is what we don't see that stimulates our interest. (How did they do that?) If the audience sees a wall with a door, and sink, and refrigerator, it will stop thinking with its imagination and just observe without actively participating. At the first sign of a flimsy door made of cardboard, or a sink that doesn't run water, the audience will focus on the artifice of the stage and be taken out of the world of the play. Let film and TV do what they do best, and let the theatre do what it does best: stimulate the imagination.

The Groundplan

Groundplans are essential to the blocking and overall staging of the play. As a director, I am bound hand and foot to having an effective groundplan. With your scene designer (if you have one), it is wise to sit in your theatre space, where the actual performances will take place, and try to envision the play as an audience member would by going over the script in your mind, scene by scene, and figuring out not only the visual qualities of the text, but also the practical considerations. Your groundplan will serve as the principal tool in communicating what the set and its movement patterns will be like before your set arrives. You do not have to sit at home with salt and pepper shakers, moving them around on the table, to block the play, but you must be able to understand how the groundplan will affect the movement patterns of the actors.

Every theatre space has its own personality. Some are more flexible than others. The following elements become important when considering your groundplan: furniture, levels/platforms, walls, fragmented scenery, and places to sit, stand, or lie down.

FURNITURE

Decide which pieces are essential to your production. Cluttering the stage with useless, decorative furniture is a waste of time and money. Never put anything on stage that is not essential to the action of the play. If a chair is necessary, make sure you know why. Will the dramatic action necessitate this chair? This sounds minor, but can lead you into trouble down the road. When directing Pinter's *The Birthday Party*, I felt it was essential that Stanley be interrogated while seated. The two interrogators gain their power over Stanley by towering over him as he is trapped in a huge overstuffed armchair. He is emotionally beaten down and is physically swallowed up by the chair and hidden from view from the audience by the end of the interrogation. In fact, sitting and standing became a metaphor for power exchanges between characters throughout the play. All of the movement revolved around the characters' relationship to furniture and how it gave them psychological power over other characters.

A helpful hint about furniture placement: Furniture should be placed on a diagonal (from the audience's point of view). This creates dynamic movement patterns, and actors are not trapped having to face out to the audience. It is very awkward for an actor to be speaking or listening to another character by craning his neck around 180 degrees in order to see the person.

In a play such as *The Dragon*, no furniture is required and the entire play can be staged without a single chair or table. Having everyone stand around constantly, however, can get tedious. In outdoor scenes, benches, boulders, and trees can act as furniture and can create different levels for the actors to play on.

LEVELS/PLATFORMS

Levels and platforms can help create dynamic staging and can be very helpful to a director for depicting environments. The problem with using them concerns safety. Safety is the main factor, but building strong and durable platforms is far more difficult and time consuming than you might imagine. As a director, I always test out any and all scenery for blocking choices. I would never make an actor do anything I wouldn't do. If you cannot build a strong and durable platform, do not use one. Risking injury is never worthwhile. There is nothing more heartbreaking than to see an actor hurt by faulty scenery. Your job as director is to look after the welfare of the actors. You or the stage manager should always check scenery for safety throughout rehearsals and performances. Never take a chance that something is safe just because it worked once. Putting actors in jeopardy is totally inexcusable.

WALLS

As stated earlier, walls are common scenery for rooms and certain exteriors, but if you can do without them, please do. Solid walls (ones that won't fall down or look rickety) are complex to build and must be maintained. You can create the illusion of walls with simple black curtains, door frames, and especially, actor movement. Once the idea of a wall is established and maintained by the actors, the audience will accept it as such. In the production of *Miss Jairus*, we created the effect of a walled-in courtyard by surrounding the actors with audience members, hence using the audience as walls. This created a human barrier, and the aisles that went through the audience created exits and entrances for the actors. Take my advice: Avoid walls! I can't tell you how many times I've seen walls collapse or be on the verge of collapse. It is unsafe and looks terrible.

FRAGMENTED SCENERY

Sometimes walls and ceiling can be fragmented (only part of the wall or ceiling is seen) to suggest a barrier or scenic element, rather than having a full-blown structure on stage. This is done to represent the fact that a certain piece of scenery exists and is a simpler way of indicating the whole picture.

PLACES TO SIT, STAND, AND LIE DOWN

The most important aspect of scenery or set dressing is the creation of a functional, as well as decorative, atmosphere for the action of the play. Overpowering scenery or decorative clutter can hinder the smooth flow of the action and can actually create impossible staging problems. If you need three exits, on and off stage, make sure they exist on the groundplan. It is absolutely essential that scenery be functional. Before anyone designs or builds anything, make sure that you have everything that you need and that the script requires. For example, if there is a big fight scene, there must be enough room on the set to stage this action. If the script requires action to happen on the floor, make sure your staging can be seen from the audience. Remember: Anything that happens on the floor can be seen easily when no one is sitting in the audience, but when heads are in the way, any action on the floor (and sometimes just sitting down) will be lost to people in the back rows. If the audience is "raked" (on a floor slanted upward, away from the stage), this is less of a problem. If your theatre space is not equipped with such raked platforming for the audience, you will have to build or buy platforming for the stage so that the action is raised above the audience's eye level. I have missed many scenes because the action was happening on the floor and I could not see it. If it is a small theatre space, the problem is sometimes worse, not better, because audience members are usually close together and anyone behind the first row of seats will have trouble seeing action on the stage. You must adjust to the demands of the space in which you are working. In the next section, I explain the types of theatre spaces that you may encounter and their effects on the audiences' perception of the play.

The Proscenium

The proscenium stage places the audience members in front of the stage, as if they are looking at a picture frame. Although this is a very common configuration, it can be deceptively difficult to use. The proscenium can make it difficult to create dynamic movement patterns and realistic staging. The physical relationship to the audience is such that actors are forced to "cheat out" (actors stand with their bodies turned out at an angle instead of being profile to the audience) and present themselves in unnatural positions. The proscenium stage can be the worst for sight lines, especially for anyone seated to the extreme left or right of the stage. I have seen many proscenium stages with extensions built out into the audience to bridge the gap between audience and actors. Old auditoriums, which are almost always proscenium stages, are notorious for this and usually have terrible acoustics as well, because the action is far from the audience and all of the sound disappears into the fly space above the actors' heads. Proscenium staging is usually better for, but not exclusive to, box set plays wherein the action was created to be in a picture frame.

The Three-Quarter Thrust

Shakespeare's theatre was a three-quarter thrust, in which the audience surrounded three quarters of the actual stage playing area. The Greek theatre had the audience surrounding the stage in a semicircle. We tend to forget that the proscenium stage was designed for theatre styles that developed during the nineteenth century. Plays written during the 1920s, 1930s, and 1940s were styled for the proscenium stage. Classical drama, however, often took place in the three-quarter-thrust format. It was with the 1960's theatre revolution that the stage and audience spaces were combined, and the action was brought into the audience. Today's director has to take these changes in staging into account and determine which is the most appropriate for her play. For what kind of stage was this play written? How can it be adapted to another format?

The thrust stage provides a happy medium between the proscenium and in-the-round staging. The idea of the thrust is to get the majority of the audience as close to the action as possible. The thrust creates a more intimate relationship between audience and actor. The audience surrounds the playing area, and the emphasis is placed on small scenic pieces that can create the required environment without obscuring the view of the audience. Your staging options are more numerous with the thrust. The potential for actors to "cheat" to the front of the stage is minimized, and more movement patterns become available to you.

In-the-Round

With in-the-round staging, the audience surrounds the stage. Exits are usually found at four equidistant intervals around the playing space. In-the-round can be very effective for the right kind of play. If you wish to give the audience the feeling of being involved directly in the action, without actually being "in" it, this is a good format for you. If you have to play in a space in which there is no formal stage, surrounding the center of the room with the audience creates a stage space in which to work. In-the-round is a very good choice for staging plays in classrooms or small spaces. You can create a space and audience that fits the needs of your play simply by arranging chairs to surround the playing space. In essence, you are creating the actual stage. Because the audience surrounds the action, in-the-round staging can maximize the stage area while creating only two or three rows of chairs, which can make it easier for the audience to see. Very little scenery is necessary because large scenic pieces will block the action from certain portions of the audience. Low furniture pieces and set dressings are usually used to establish the scene, while the space is defined by the audience's relationship to the action. Another variation on the in-the-round staging is the creation of stage space with audience seating in cross shapes or T shapes. For example, if the audience sits in four corners and leaves space for two wide aisles that intersect, your stage space is now in the shape of a crossroads.

If you keep directing, you are bound to run into all of these styles of staging. You should be familiar with all of them, because the only way to understand the various advantages and disadvantages of these spaces is to work in them. Directing is about experience. Many problems you encounter while directing cannot be foreseen. All you can hope to do is be as prepared as possible, so that you can be ready to problem-solve "on your feet."

Blocking

It will become obvious to you what kind of movement, or blocking, works best for the space you are in. A good groundplan will guide you in making blocking choices. Movement patterns are affected greatly by placement of scenery and set pieces. One big mistake that beginning directors make with blocking is assuming that movement is the be-all and end-all. Movement must be motivated by the action and dialogue of the play. Creating pretty stage pictures or making actors move only to "break it up" is completely unnecessary if your staging corresponds to the demands of the text. Don't make arbitrary, "stagey" choices. Go to the text of the play and make your decisions according to what the text indicates. Then, try it out in rehearsal. You will be able to tell if it works when you see it in action.

I refuse to give charts and diagrams concerning how to block a play. There are no rules. Your own good judgement should guide you. Ninety percent of directing is being able to problem-solve during rehearsals. Blocking comes out of the *action* of the play. The spatial relationship of objects and furniture can be derived from what the characters do and what relationship they have to each other. Creating physical obstacles between characters can create the dynamics necessary for emotional and physical stage action.

Creating stage blocking is a lot like creating choreography. You are creating movement patterns that develop tensions and rhythms between actors and between their environments. Go to see a dance performance. Whether it is modern, ballet, or jazz, its choreography is based on interactions between dancers. Relationships are created through wordless movement that is usually accompanied by music or sound. In a play, the words *are* the music, and the actor's movement and gestures *are* the dance. Whenever someone makes a move on stage, it has to be grounded in stage action. What is that person doing? Why are they moving? Where are they going? And most importantly, what will happen next? It is the anticipation of forwarding action that creates audience interest. A move is created in order to engage the audience's attention.

As an example, I directed a new play entitled *Empties* wherein I created an entire movement collage at the beginning of the play. Two of the characters were making a sculpture on stage. The characters had been working at it for so long that the routine of building it had taken over their movements. The actors and I created a choreography in which the getting of materials for the sculpture and the handing of them back and forth made rhythmic patterns like a machine in motion. The actors' movements were precise, focused, and followed a set pattern. This created a sense of anticipation from the audience as they wondered how this action had developed. It was exciting to watch and engage the spectator's sense of wonder as to when this movement would change or stop and when the characters would speak, essentially, "What will happen next?" This all happened before the dialogue had even begun and created a rhythm and tension that reflected the action that the rest of the play would follow.

This choreography was not worked out beforehand. I did not sit at home and write down the movements of the actors or move salt shakers around a model of the set. These patterns were created in rehearsal with the actors; they developed out of the relationships between the characters and the actors' responses to each other. Certain moves were indicative of the way a character walked or used his hands. For example, the manic character of Dino had a rhythmic way of throwing things over his shoulder without looking where they were going to land. This said a lot about Dino's self-absorption and his lack of concern for what and who was around him. Again, these moves came out of rehearsal, from an understanding of what the characters would do and how they would do it.

Again, I refer to dance and choreography as a way of understanding patterns of movement. Also, studying the behavior of animals can be a fascinating way to depict the movement of characters. I have seen the eighteenth-century comedy of manners, *The School for Scandal*, rehearsed and performed with movement and blocking fashioned after various animals. (Some of the characters actually have animal names; for example, Mr. Snake.) This created an exciting choreography that became a style of movement, but also reflected the personalities of the characters. Especially in the case of "period" plays in which there is a certain style associated with the text, a director can avoid empty clichés. It is too easy to fall into the trap of classical acting. A director must develop a style with the actors. Again, animal, dance, and ritualistic movement often can help the actors find a way into the style of the play.

The stage trafficking of a play is a large part of the director's work, and it comes out of the rehearsal process. The director's job is to create, from what he sees, interesting patterns of action that reflect the conflict and tensions within the characters from moment to moment, and how those moments build during the course of the play as a whole.

So, You Need a Cast for Your Play? 5

A uditions are always a difficult prospect for actors and director alike. Trying to make decisions on which actor to choose and which actor to cast in which role can be especially painful. The choices are easier, of course, when you are familiar with the actors and understand their capabilities. But if you've never worked with them, or if it's your first time directing, this can be a stressful experience. There is really nothing you can do to make it more pleasant other than provide the actors, and yourself, with a relaxed atmosphere. For this, your stage manager can be of great help to you by being prepared and calm.

Preparation for Casting

As the director, you should be familiar with each and every character in the play and have an idea of what qualities you think the character should possess. This is not to say you should be locked into looking for a specific physical type of actor (because he or she may not exist), but you must know the character you are casting well enough to discuss it with the potential actors to see if you can communicate your ideas to them. It is extremely important to be able to relate to and work with the actors who are auditioning. Get to know them. After an initial reading, and if you like how they read, ask them questions about themselves and their interest in the play. Get to know their ideas about the play and the characters. In this way you can see if they are prepared and serious about auditioning and being cast. It is always better to cast an actor who is excited and serious about the play than one who gives a strong audition but is indifferent or even downright rude in his presentation of himself and his attitude toward being in the play.

All that you can really tell from a "cold" reading of the script is whether a person has any acting ability. Once you have an idea that she can act, sit down and talk with her; get to know a little bit about her and her intentions about being in the play. This can prevent a lot of confusion and hardship later on if you find out that you have an uncommitted actor on your hands. You cast her, so there is no way of backing out without a lot of embarrassment on your part, not to mention the time wasted and having to replace someone as opening night gets closer and closer.

CALMNESS AND KINDNESS

There is nothing worse than a rude or abusive director. Do not abuse your power. Actors are under a lot of pressure. They are extremely nervous, so putting them at ease will benefit not only them, but also yourself. Someone who is nervous will sense any hostility, and although he may be a fine actor, he will not give a very good audition. Remember, actors are auditioning you as well! You may miss a good casting choice because of an audition environment that is unfriendly or chaotic.

Have a stage manager or assistant stage manager greet the actors and sign them in while they are waiting to audition. If the actors arrive and see someone is there waiting to assist them and give them any necessary information (such as sample scenes to look over or character descriptions and information about rehearsal times and performance dates), they will see that you and your production staff are serious and have a professional attitude. Make sure you and your staff are on time and on schedule. Actors resent (and rightfully so) auditions that are run inefficiently and make them wait around longer than is necessary.

I will never forget an audition at a theatre where, on arrival, I walked into an auditorium filled with actors and proceeded to sit around for two hours while I waited to read a two-minute scene. I then waited to see if I would be asked to read again, only to be told, another hour later, that the audition was over. Because there was no sign-up sheet and no explanation from the director or stage manager about how the audition was being handled, the actors simply had to wait and *see* what would happen. There was no way of knowing what the director wanted, nor the amount of time that would be spent waiting. As a result, I never went back and also advised other actors to stay away. Actors, out of politeness, may put up with any rudeness that you or your staff inflict on them, but they will not take you seriously, and if you make the mistake of being rude to someone you are casting, they may behave the same way to you during rehearsals. Remember, if you do not treat people professionally, you cannot expect to be treated professionally in return.

Setting Up the Casting Schedule

COLD READINGS

The most common way to audition nonprofessional actors is the cold reading. The actors do not need to prepare in advance (except to read the play). They simply read preselected scenes from the script "cold" (without preparation). Making the text available will save you and the actors a lot of time and energy: the actors will not be stumbling through an unfamiliar text, and you will not have to take the time to explain the scene and character with each auditioner. One of the problems with cold readings is that some actors simply do not read well cold. If possible, let actors get familiar with the material before an audition.

Create a list of characters and character descriptions that conveys how you envision the roles. This will help the actors not only understand the play, but also let them see what you want in casting; you will save a lot of time not discussing the characters. You will not waste your and their time discussing roles that are not right for them. During your callbacks, when you know you're serious about casting someone, you can take more time to discuss character and other issues.

PREPARED MONOLOGUES

Prepared monologues are used most often in professional auditions, but they can help students understand the "real world" of casting. By having the actors prepare a monologue (about two minutes in length) in the style of the play you have chosen (comedy, drama, mystery, etc.), you can get an idea of how an actor handles a speech that she has prepared and practiced in advance. This can also be an indicator of how serious the students are. For beginners, however, a prepared monologue can be too daunting a proposition, and they may not audition. You may end up losing someone who may be interested in auditioning but is afraid of having to prepare a monologue. I would suggest this technique for students that you al- ready know—let the open audition call be geared toward readings.

IMPROVISATION AND AUDITIONS

Improvisation can be a very useful technique for casting purposes. Improvisation gives the director a chance to see actors respond and make choices based on their instincts and impulses. It's a way to see if an actor, particularly one you are unsure about casting, not only can read the lines well, but also can take your direction and come up with ideas of her own, based on whatever information she is given at the moment. Improvisation also tests the actor's awareness of what is going on around her, and how she relates to the other actors on the stage. Can the actor pick up on what another actor is doing and work with that? Or is she stuck in her own world and unresponsive to the others? Because theatre is a live event, and the energies and circum- stances of each performance vary from night to night, it is important that the actors can "think on their feet." What happens if, God forbid, an actor drops a line or jumps a cue? Is the other actor in the scene so locked in to what she is doing that she cannot get things back on track and "cover" for the mistake? I remember one of the first produc- tions I ever directed, *The Fifth of July*, in which an actor went "blank" and could not think of her next line. Although quite talented and well rehearsed, she simply lost her place for a moment quite by chance. Unfortunately, the other actors in the scene did not know where to go next, and an excruciatingly long pause ensued (perhaps it was only a few seconds, but on stage and in front of an audience, it seemed like ten minutes). Luckily, a skilled actor trained in improvisation, who was supposed to enter in the very next moment, came on and saved the day by adjusting to the situation and saying a line that brought the scene back to its place.

Whether amateur or professional, actors are imperfect and something unexpected is bound to happen. This can make the the- atre experience exciting, but the probability of a missed entrance or sound cue is quite high. An actor must be prepared for this inevita- bility, and improvisation is one way of testing whether an actor can respond quickly in a crisis.

Improvisation is also a great way to see what kind of imagination the actor has. If you give the actor a specific action to play, can she pick up on it and make something from your direction? Will the actor balk and try to rationalize and avoid the direction, or go with the process and *try* things. In my experience, even when someone is known as a talented actor, if you cannot communicate with her and get her to break her old habits by trying something new, the rehearsal process can be stale and stagnant. In order to keep performances fresh and alive, it is important to know that the actor will make strong choices and take chances, even at the risk of seeming foolish. More information on improvisation techniques is provided in Chapter 7.

Scheduling Auditions

There are several ways to set up audition times. First, you must decide how many days to allow for general auditions and how many for people you want to call back.

Usually, general auditions take two days, so that someone who can't make it one day will have another chance to audition. It is a good idea to have callbacks on one day, so that you can mix and match actors and have them audition with each other to see how the overall cast will look and act together.

Auditions can be grueling for both actors and directors, so it is usually wise to make them as short and concise as possible. Three hours (including breaks) is probably as much as anyone can handle. After hours of watching auditions, you will become numb to new auditioners, so don't drag it out if at all possible. Make sure the scenes and monologues you have preselected are short but have enough "meat" to allow you to see what the actor can do. Usually, you can tell in the first few minutes whether you are interested in a certain actor.

After you have spent some time directing, the first few *seconds* of an audition will probably give you what you need to see. Use the callback time to have your potential cast try the scene in different ways, perhaps with different physical gestures or involvement in some activity that counterpoints the dialogue. Save your concentrated time for actors about whom you are serious. If you wish to give all of your auditioners a chance to learn from their auditions, (for example, what they can do better), be prepared to spend a lot of time with them. Giving them the "bum's rush" will probably discourage them from ever auditioning again. So, determine the nature of your audition and give yourself enough time to deal properly with each auditioner. Whether you want it to be a learning experience for further auditioning skills or a more professional look at the world of auditioning determines the nature of your audition.

The "Cattle Call," or the Open Audition ■ In an open audition, all of the actors are placed in the same room or hall at the same appointed time and must wait and watch everyone else audition. Having the auditioners sign in and wait to be called to read, either waiting in the same room or called in individually, is up to you. I prefer to have the actors wait outside the audition room so they can practice the scene they will read, and then call them in in pairs (or as many as are required for a scene; hopefully not more than four at a time). Having everyone in the same room watch auditions can be hazardous. Once an actor gives a good audition and elicits a favorable response (usually from her friends), other auditioners may be discouraged or try to imitate what they just saw. Also, the first people to audition have the disadvantage of not being able to see the scene played out. It is always better if the actor is fresh and raring to go. You also can deal with the auditioners more comfortably if you get individual time with them, thus not having to censor what you say in front of the other actors (especially if you are interested in or happen to know the auditioner). Everyone should be as comfortable as possible.

Predetermined Time Slots ■ Another way to set up auditions is with a timetable of audition slots on which actors sign up for specific periods of no more than ten to fifteen minutes. Again, this is a professional technique, but saves time and energy in the long run. The schedule is set and no one will have to sit around for hours waiting to audition. I believe this is the best and most efficient way for both the actors and the director.

The following is a sample timetable:

Sunday, February 17th

7:00–7:15PM	*Sukie Jones*
7:15–7:30	*Slawomir Mrozek*
7:30–7:45	*Steven Tyler*
7:45–8:00	*Sally Yellowtree*
8:00–8:15	*Break*
8:15–8:30	*Angel Rodriquez*

Though not shown here, the timetable continues for the duration of the time allotted. Using this method enables you to know how many actors to expect, and they will know how much time they will have to be at the audition. Also, you will know if you will get all girls and one boy (or the other way around), and so start a campaign to get more boys to audition (or more girls).

You may wish to allot special time slots for singers and dancers if you are doing a musical production. You will need an accompanist and a piano, unless you wish to hear the singers a capella. A similar timetable can be set up and auditions held at a time and day separate from the acting audition.

The most important thing here is to keep to the time schedule so that you do not waste people's time and get actors upset with you. A good stage manager will keep you and the auditioners on schedule so that you can concentrate on watching and listening to the auditions and not worry about what's going on in the hall during any particular audition. A stage manager is invaluable during auditions for keeping them running smoothly and efficiently. The less the director has to worry about, the better. You will have plenty to worry about just getting the right cast together.

The Audition Form

Shown here is an example of an audition form that can be used to gather the information necessary to create an effective cast and rehearsal schedule.

Production Title: *The Dragon*
Performance Dates: May 19, 20, 21 (evenings at 8:00)
Rehearsal Dates: April 11–May 18 (four times a week for three hours, M–Th afternoons)
Acting Experience: Role: Play: Theatre/School:
Special Skills: (i.e., fencing, sports, gymnastics, dance, singing, musical instrument ability)
Scheduling Conflicts:

Callbacks

Callbacks are an important time for the director. At this time, you have the actors you are serious about casting. Use the time wisely. Have ready the scenes or monologues you want each actor to read. Know which characters you want to pair with which actors, and give the actors as much information as possible about what you expect from them. Have the actor try a scene in different ways, with different intentions, even if he is not necessarily what you initially envision for the character. You want to see if the actor will respond to your direction, and how he can work with what you give him as direction. Have these things in mind before the callback so that you can audition actors more efficiently while they are standing in front of you. You will be expected to talk about characterization and what the characters are doing in the scene. Again, sit down with them and ask them questions about the play, their characters, or why they are interested in auditioning. This will give you an idea of what it will be like to work with the actors in rehearsal. If they are difficult *now*, look out—rehearsals will be even worse! Your job is tough enough without having people argue with you all along the way, so get to know these actors. Once you've cast them, you're stuck with them!

Alternative Casting

Try not to focus on the actor's looks. Acting is about portraying a fictional character. Typecasting is unnecessary and can rule out actors who might be excellent for a certain role but who never get the chance to read for it because they don't look "right." The same thing goes for someone who may look right but can't do the part. Remember, makeup and costumes can transform an actor physically, so don't depend on looks. Get the right actor who can "act" the role, not just look like it.

The theatre has great potential for nontraditional casting. Casting choices are too often based on the age, gender, race and looks of the actor. What do we mean by *alternative casting*? This terminology has taken on many and varied interpretations, but my feeling is that alternative casting is that which does not produce clichéd or stereotyped roles simply because of the traditional ethnic or gender-based heritage of those roles. Because of the nature of theatre, a director can cast in a variety of ways that are not open to, for example, a film or television casting director. *Acting* is just what the term implies; it is about acting and creating a character. Casting productions according to race and gender is unnecessary. There is no reason why King Lear's daughters should be of the same ethnicity, nor do they need to look like they come from the same family. What is important is the actor's abilities, and what these abilities can bring to a given role. It is the actor's work to make a character come to life.

Classical texts are easily accessible to alternative casting. A handsome, young, white male actor is not a requirement for playing Hamlet or Romeo. Conversely, this same actor should be open to character roles not traditionally available to him, such as Caliban or Malvolio. Stanley Kowalski does not need to be played by a Marlon Brando look-alike. Although Brando originated the role, had James Earl Jones been cast initially, we would now associate the role with him instead.

Theatre is about transformations and imagination, not only of time and place but also of characters. The audience's imagination is engaged in the actor's portrayal and transformation into the character. It is a creative challenge for the actor and often brings out nuances in the character that have not previously been explored. The bottom line is that your vision of the play should include a wide variety of interpretations and that actors are capable of doing more than their outward appearances indicate.

So, Now that You've Got a Cast, What Do You Do? 6

6

Breaking Down the Script for Rehearsals

Before any work can be done in rehearsal, the director must prepare a rehearsal game plan. What will you do in rehearsal? This is a question that the actors will be asking and expecting you to answer. An actor is always looking to the director for guidance throughout the rehearsal process. The objective is to guide the actor toward her final performance. As the final technical rehearsals are approaching, the actor should have gained the necessary confidence throughout the rehearsal process to play the role. She reaches a point at which the director is no longer necessary, because she has completed the work necessary to portray the character on her own. This is what the rehearsal process is about: discovering the character within the actor and giving the actor the confidence and strength necessary to go on stage in front of an audience and play the character to the best of her abilities. The director is the audience throughout the rehearsal process. Actors cannot see what they are doing from the inside, so it is up to the director to get them to see what does and does not work for the character. The rehearsal process is a time to explore and try different approaches to creating the most effective performance. Rehearsals, however, are not performances. Rehearsals should give the actor a chance to discover what is most effective. A character evolves *from* the rehearsal process. There is no predetermined model to fulfill. Every actor is different and brings different qualities to the role. It is the director's job to bring these qualities out of the individual and to create a character for the first time.

The rehearsal process should be used as a time for getting the qualities of the actor to meld with those of the character. A director's job is to help the actor discover what *he* can bring to the character. Unfortunately, some directors often cast an actor and then try to mold him into their vision of the character, trying to get the actor to play the role as *they* would play it. The director must work with the actor to discover the character, not force some preconceived notion on the actor. Use rehearsal time to try various approaches with the actor. Guide the actor in the direction that his work naturally takes him. An actor must make choices based on his knowledge of the text and his understanding of the world of the play. Directors should guide the actor and shape his performance based on these choices, discovering with the actor what "works" for the character and the play as a whole.

Act and Scene Breakdowns

What are act and scene breakdowns, and how do you determine where they are? What is the significance of act and scene breakdowns? Traditionally, act breaks signal the moment of climax where the action has come to a head and can be resolved only by a major shift in the events of the play. The action of each act has built to a point of release. Naturally, the release for earlier acts of the play builds toward the grand climax at the end of the final act. Scene breaks are moments of action within the individual acts that build the action and create conflicts that bring us to the final moment of release in tension at the climax of each separate act.

If you think of a play as a musical piece, each instrument within the whole group of instruments plays off of the others to create rhythms and tensions that move the music forward. Imagine music that remained static and did not build in intensity—pretty boring. All music moves toward the crescendo that has been built up throughout the composition. A play needs to be composed in the same way: It needs to build in intensity and rhythm. If a musical composition lacks this movement and build, the listener is not carried along and does not become involved in the music. A play is a journey that takes the audience somewhere. The director's job is to break down the script and create a score out of the words through stage action. Each scene must have an action, a place to go, that builds up to the final moment at which the audience is brought to its final revelation and destination. This scene breakdown not only is a way to rehearse the play in manageable units, but also aids the director in finding the conflicts and tensions that create the forward motion of the play.

Because a play is a compilation of scenes building to a climactic scene, you are looking for scenes that can be rehearsed in and of themselves. Usually scenes begin or end when a character makes an entrance or an exit. This signals where a scene begins and ends. In Molière's theatre, new scenes were marked each time a new character came into a scene. The expression *French scene* comes from this tradition. A play concerns the relationship between and conflicts of its characters. These are found in scenes between characters. Each scene has its own life and action, and this is where the rehearsal reveals these actions. Do your homework: You must take the time to discover the action of each scene before you begin to rehearse. Where does this scene bring us? What has happened just before this scene, and how does it affect what is happening in this scene, and how will it affect the events of the next scene?

I will now begin referring to a one-act play by Paul Day, entitled *The Dragon*. I will also refer to this play in discussing other aspects of the rehearsal process.

Think of a play whose action starts from a point of stasis that is interrupted by something that happens and forces its characters into doing something. This stasis is usually established before the time of the play begins. In *The Dragon*, Cass and her mother and father are living in a small town, running a family business. This stasis happens before the play even begins. Then Cass's mother is killed accidentally, although Cass thinks it was murder. Here is where our play begins. All of this has happened before the first words are spoken. This is what sets off the action of the entire play. The actors must understand this action before they can begin to be involved in the conflict of the first scene between Cass's and her father. Cass mourns the loss of her mother and wants revenge against "the Dragon" that has "killed" her mother. Her father, mourning the loss of his wife, throws himself into his work to hide from the pain of it and consequently takes his grief and frustration out on his daughter. Cass takes this as a sign of a lack of love from her father, and this creates the conflict that sets off the journey of the play.

The journey of the play is in Cass's discovering that the loss of her mother is a part of her life that she cannot control but must come to grips with by herself. By "killing" her fear and rage through the murder of the Dragon, she realizes that an eye for an eye is not the way to solve her problems. Cass must look to the living world and the people in it (her father and Josh), and most importantly, to her own willpower and sense of self to continue with her life after the loss of her mother.

The Journey of the Play

As a director, I find "the journey" of the play to be a major insight into the directing of it. Every play takes us somewhere. Plays that remain stagnant are deadly and untheatrical. Whether the journey is a character's evolution/quest or a movement of time, place, and action of an entire community of characters, this journey creates the action of the play. I am not speaking necessarily of plot line or story. An emotional/sensory journey for the character(s) can be a factor in reaching the audience on a gut level. Think of your play as a series of roads or paths that lead you somewhere. Now think of yourself (the director) as an audience member. What moves you? Where would you like to be taken? What adventures would you like to take? What choices go into selecting a certain road, and how do those choices change/evolve or how does circumstance/chance/fate guide you and change your choices along the way? See yourself as a Robert Frost character who is standing at the fork in the road. Which road do you take? The most interesting road is the one "less traveled by." You are leading an audience down a road that will take them somewhere, hopefully somewhere new and exciting. Think of yourself as showing someone a new way of seeing that place. This is the job of the director. You are an emotional/psychological/physical tour guide. Make their journey exciting. (Refer to the 28 steps listed in Chapter 3.)

A typical journey can be like the one in *The Dragon*. The "journey" of the play is Cass's discovery that you become what you fear. To put it into one clear, concise phrase: facing your fear(s). Now you can see the shape that the play must take. We need to guide the audience through Cass's journey, and her discovery becomes the *audience's* discovery. It should be as exciting and evocative for the audience as it is for Cass.

Once you start to understand the purpose and placement of each scene, you can start to build the structure of the whole play. Create a list of scenes and which characters are involved. Figure out the main action in each scene and what every character "wants." For example, Cass wants revenge for the death of her mother. How does she go about getting it? By confronting and attempting to kill the Dragon. Does she achieve this? Is she stopped by anything or anybody along the way? Who? What? How does this affect the outcome of her quest to kill the Dragon? What does she learn from attempting her quest? You must do this for all of the scenes and characters in order to understand the play and its ultimate shape, and how you will ultimately stage the action of the play. This is for you to research and decide.

WHERE TO BEGIN?

The following is a breakdown of scenes from Paul Day's play *The Dragon*, with how they can be rehearsed in a five-week period. This can be modified according to rehearsal time allotted, and to the length and complexity of the particular show.

First, break down the script into manageable scenes for rehearsal. The following is a scene list that outlines all of the scenes of the play and who appears in them.

THE DRAGON SCENE BREAKDOWN

Scene 1 (pp. 1–7)
Cass, Giacomo (her father)
    Life at the print shop. Cass and her father are mourning the death of Cass's mother.

Scene 2 (pp. 7–11)
Giacomo, Robert
    Giacomo and Robert discuss Robert's impending wedding and the accidental death of Cass's mother.

Scene 3 (pp. 11–12)
Cass
    Cass has a monologue in which she reveals that she does not believe that the death of her mother was an accident and wishes to avenge her death.

Scene 4 (pp. 12–15)
Cass, Josh
    Cass describes her plan for revenge (to kill the Dragon) to her friend Josh.

Scene 5 (pp. 15–23)
Cass, Josh, Fox
    Introduction of the Fox, who tries to persuade Cass not to go through with her plan. Both Fox and Josh are against her plan for revenge.

Scene 6 (pp. 23–24)
Fox

A monologue in which the Fox tells about the legend of the Dragon, and how anyone who kills the Dragon becomes the Dragon as well.

Scene 7 (pp. 24–27)
Father, Robert

Cass's father and his friend Robert are looking for Cass, who they think has run away and is lost.

Scene 8 (pp. 27–28)
Cass

A monologue in which Cass discovers the Dragon's lair and shows her fear about confronting the Dragon.

Scene 9 (pp. 28–36)
Cass, Dragon

The fight between Cass and the Dragon, in which Cass kills the Dragon and becomes the Dragon by assuming his mask.

Scene 10 (pp. 36–40)
Josh, Giacomo

Josh goes back to tell Cass's father what has happened, and how Cass has become the Dragon. Giacomo believes she is dead.

Scene 11 (pp. 40–47)
Josh, Fox
Josh tries to get the Fox to help him rescue Cass from her fate.

Scene 12 (pp. 47–49)
Cass (as the Dragon), Josh

Josh tries to confront Cass and tell her what she's done. Josh gets scared and runs away.

Scene 13 (pp. 49–52)
Josh, Fox
Josh tries to get the Fox to help him break the spell on Cass.

Scene 14 (pp. 52–59)
Cass (as Dragon), Josh, Fox

The climactic battle where Josh confronts Cass and breaks the spell by declaring his love for her (with the help of the Fox).

Scene 15 (pp. 59–end)
Cass, Giacomo

Cass is reunited with her father and finally comes to accept the death of her mother as an accident.

Now you can break down the play for rehearsal. You need to build each scene in rehearsal, scene by scene, in order to create the whole. As each separate scene becomes fully realized, you can start to put together whole sections of the play, and then finally run through the whole play from beginning to end without interruption.

SAMPLE REHEARSAL SCHEDULE FOR *THE DRAGON*

Week 1. Read-through of the play.

Discussion of characters and environment (sets, lights, costumes). Getting the cast to know and work with each other.

Week 2. Rehearse scenes 1–5.

Rehearse each scene separately. Run through all five scenes in sequence at the end of the week.

Week 3. Rehearse scenes 5–10.

Rehearse each scene separately. Run through scenes 1–10, working on individual problems of character and staging. Provide notes.

Week 4. Rehearse scenes 10–15.

Rehearse each scene separately. Run through the entire play. Work on problem scenes and monologues, providing notes.

Week 5. Run through play at least twice without stopping.

Use the last three days for technical and dress rehearsals. Try to have at least two to three dress rehearsals to fix any technical problems and let the actors get used to costumes in full run-throughs without stopping. Give notes afterward.

Opening Night!

So, What Happens in Rehearsal Anyway?

7

Once the script is broken down and a rehearsal schedule set, then what?

The First Reading

This is a very exciting and important time for the director. At this time, you discuss your ideas and vision of the play with the actors and answer any questions they may have, after they have had a chance to read through the play out loud as a cast.

Create a pleasant atmosphere. Consider providing refreshments and snacks—actors are always hungry. Your expectations of the actors should not be unreasonably high, because they are nervous and will probably not read at their best. Remember, there have been no rehearsals, so do not expect full-blown performances until opening night.

Let the stage manager begin by talking about rehearsal schedules, timetables, being on time, costume fittings, and so forth. Let her establish that her word is law! Second only to you, she is in charge of rehearsals. Her authority must be respected. The stage manager is the direct link among actors, director, and designers. It is her responsibility to make sure communication is kept clear and open. The actors will have to depend on the stage manager if anything goes wrong, so establish this right away.

At this point, you may want to make some opening remarks about the play and put the actors at ease by letting them know that this is not a performance, but a reading to get the overall feeling of the play. I usually hold detailed comments on the play's theme, concepts, and designs until after the reading. This places fewer expectations on the actors. They won't be listening anyway; they will be too nervous about reading in front of the others. After the first reading, the actors are more relaxed and in the mood to ask questions, discuss the play, and get to know each other better.

Warming Up

Actors need to warm up their voices and get into rehearsal clothes early enough to discover any problems. Have group warm-up activities before each rehearsal to build energy, loosen up the actors, dispel nervousness, and create a good ensemble feeling. Vocal exercises such as nursery rhymes, songs, and tongue twisters are great for limbering up voices, and help the actors to concentrate on "getting into character." Movement exercises such as stretching out or doing simple dance steps can get the actors' bodies ready to go. The actors must be focused on the task at hand. Get someone in the cast to lead these exercises (alternating different leaders). Have the leaders come up with their own warm-ups. This encourages variety and helps stimulate imaginations. Remember, even "pros" have to warm up. Concentration and focus are the keys to a successful performance.

The First Week of Rehearsals

Rehearsals should be a process of growth for the actors and production team alike. Actors need time to grow into their characters and to try different approaches and choices that you can't foresee until you get to work in rehearsal. Don't try to mold the actors into your personal conception, but work with what the actor can bring to the character. This can be more interesting than your original idea. You must know where you want to end up and make sure the choices that are made make sense within the script and the context of the play, but don't force actors to be who they are not. Trying to make them play what you want is a waste of time. Rehearsal is a collaborative process during which ideas and choices change and evolve, guided by the director's vision. Use the first two weeks of rehearsal to explore the play and its characters with the actors.

Every actor will have different energies and different ways of rehearsing, just by virtue of the fact that they are individuals with different backgrounds and points of view. Use this time to get to know the actors and how they work best. Some will ask questions and want to talk about characters right away, while others will prefer to try things and stay quiet, and then ask questions after they've explored a little bit.

The idea is to enable the actor to find the character. The only way to do that is to take chances and try different approaches. I spent three weeks rehearsing for *Rosencrantz and Guildenstern are Dead*. I had all the technical aspects of the character down (proper voice, movement, look, etc.) but not the *life*. I was playing The Leading Player, who was, in my oversimplified view, a hammy, histrionic actor. This view was to change, however, with a simple note from the director during the last week of rehearsal. He told me to enjoy being the flamboyant actor, to have fun with the character, and to understand that acting was the major joy of living for the character. This finally made the character fall into place for me. A performance that looked like it was headed for disaster took shape and played very well. This type of problem is one that cannot be foreseen. If you realize, however, that a rehearsal is a series of building blocks that you are fitting together, and that they take form as rehearsals go along, you will not frustrate yourself or the actor by trying to get results immediately. An actor needs time to assimilate every aspect and have time to *live it* in rehearsal. By giving the character "life time," the characters are literally born, then develop from adolescence to adulthood. After all, you are creating a living human being on stage, and the personality of the character must have time to be nurtured, live, and grow.

What Do You Actually Do in Rehearsal Anyway?

According to the needs of the script, rehearsal time can be used in different ways. Some directors like to rehearse with only the script and use very little in the way of improvisation away from the text, theatre games, or exercises. They will keep rehearsing scenes and finding new approaches and ways of playing those scenes. I enjoy working this way. I like to approach all of the scenes in as many ways as possible by watching them live on stage. You will never use everything from every rehearsal, but you will find different bits and pieces that do work. I like to use improvisation or non-script-related exercises only for specific problems, when an actor is having trouble resolving something.

Improvisation and theatre games can help to relax actors and open them up to new experiences. They can also be used to address specific problems in the script. For example, if a play incorporates animal characters, have the actors go to a park, forest, or zoo, study animal movements, and then design improvisations around these animal characteristics. The actors may find fresh perspectives on their characters that they might not have otherwise foreseen. Try relaxation exercises with actors who are uncomfortable with their bodies or voices. Sometimes actors are not making any character choices because they cannot free themselves from being "watched" and are looking for approval. Part of acting is taking chances. Sometimes an actor will feel foolish, but improvisations and exercises can help them get over these fears.

The following is a list of excellent books of rehearsal exercises that might be helpful.

Theatre Games, by Clive Barker
Impro: Improvisation for the Theatre, by Keith Johnstone
Improvisation for the Theatre, by Viola Spolin
200+ Ideas for Drama, by Anna Sher and Charles Verrall
Improv, by Greg Atkins

One of the director's responsibilities is to address specific acting problems that arise during rehearsal. She must identify what needs attention and how to problem-solve creatively with the actors.

The Rehearsal

It is hard to describe what actually happens in rehearsal, because actors' personalities and the demands of each play are different. The only way to learn is by doing. A director develops his "work tools" by trial and error. The following is a description of my rehearsal process.

First, we read through the scene seated, focusing on understanding the dialogue and discussing any ambiguous meanings or intentions. Then, we discuss the subtext (what is *not* being talked about) and discuss the action of the scene (what's happening to the characters). Then, the actors read the scene, moving around on the rehearsal floor, which has been taped out with the groundplan. I watch the unfocused scene, the first time letting the actors find their way through it. I never want to interrupt any natural impulses the actors might have with premature exclamations of "That's not right!" or "That doesn't work!" The next couple of times we go through the scene, I stop and start the actors. I interrupt them to make suggestions for characterization or movement choices by taking what they are doing and modifying it with specific ideas I have discerned from watching them. As we stop and start, I point out the choices the actors are making and try to focus the action. This is to ensure that the overall objective of the scene is clear from my knowledge of the total action of the play, and how this scene fits into the whole. All the choices must reflect the journey of the scene. Take time to discuss any problems the actors are having with the characters and how the scene relates to the rest of the play. Try the scene with new objectives each time—"You want to make your father laugh"; "You want to lie to your father"—always giving the actor an action to play. Start to "rough block" the scene. Try different movements and gestures that enhance the action. Run the scene a couple of times without stopping, taking notes on problem spots or character choices, and give notes after each run through. Make sure the notes are constructive and give the actor something to achieve or work toward. Giving only negative criticism will not only upset the actors, but also make them less inclined to try to work things out. You must give the actor something on which to work; in other words, a direction to go in. They cannot work in a void, and because they have no way of "seeing" themselves, it is up to the director to let them know what it is they are doing and how to improve on it.

So, How Do You Deal with the Technical and Design Aspects? 8

O utline the technical and design requirements of a play to help you avoid unwanted surprises. The first and most obvious place to look for design surprises is in the initial scene description; the second, subsequently throughout the text. Some plays will give full and detailed descriptions of what technical requirements they foresee. Other plays, however, will just state place and time, with the details left up to the director and designer. It is ultimately up to the director to determine what is necessary to the production. Remember that a play is a skeleton that must be fleshed out according to the vision of the director.

Let's take *The Dragon* as an example. The scene is described as follows:

```
Place: A Distant Village
Time: Quite a While Ago
```

Now, what could this possibly mean? Well, the possibilities are endless, indeed, but if we read on, the stage directions say the following:

```
"The play is set in front of three panels. The first
panel shows the inside of a print shop. The middle panel
is neutral. On the back hangs the canvas of the Dragon's
lair. The third panel is a forest scene. There is a
stool in front of the print shop."
```

So, we have the print shop, a Dragon's lair, and a forest scene. What is the playwright getting at here? Initial impulses might lead us to believe we are in a small village, during a time when mythical creatures such as dragons exist. But where? What village? Are all villages the same? In what time period are we? What are the characters wearing? What kind of lighting is there? None of these questions are answered in the stage directions. Even the suggested "three panels" may not be right for your production, according to your concept of the production. This is where the director and designer must start to make their own decisions about how the play will look. Again, historical paintings and maps may be helpful in deciding where to locate the play. We know that it does not take place in the present moment or in any "known" historical period, but that it does take place in a small village during a period when "print shops" still existed. The rest is to be determined by the creative team. Also, the playwright is pointing at a nonrealistic representation of the scenes by describing "panels." But what materials make up these panels? And how are the scenes represented on them? Are they drawings, photographs, or maps? This is a signpost to the overall design of the play. Are the costumes, lights, and scenery two-dimensional? Are we in a fairytale world? Are the characters cartoons or real people? And how does this affect the actors and the acting style of the play? What about makeup? Later on in the play, the character of the Dragon is wearing a mask to represent his appearance as a dragon. Cass puts on the mask when she becomes the Dragon. How does this affect the appearance of other characters? Do they all wear masks? Can we show the change in characters through changes in costumes, masks, sets, and lights? Now is the time to determine the possibilities of design and which of them will support your vision of the play.

The designs and their technical requirements are all dependent on the overall concept of the play. What kind of world are you creating? If it is an unrealistic fairytale, what does that fairytale look like? Perhaps illustrated children's books may help determine what that world looks like. This is where your associations to painting and music become important, to help designers "see" what you envision. What colors, shapes, and textures will be used? All of these are determined by your vision of the play.

Getting a Technical Staff and Stage Manager

There are always students, teachers, and early-career theatre artists who are willing to donate their time and energy to a production. The director is instrumental in getting this staff together. There is an art to getting people excited about a project. As it is important to "infect" your cast with your passion, the same goes for getting your staff's interest. There are students who are interested in gaining management and organizational skills and may wish to help you manage your production. (Not everyone is an actor.) At the same time you announce auditions, ask for volunteers to help you design and build the play. Art classes, shop classes, and home economics classes are invaluable sources of help. In-class projects that correspond to the needs of the show could perhaps be created. For example, get the home economics class to make the costumes. They need to sew something, so why not costumes? Get the art classes to paint the scenery. By involving the other parts of the school, you will lessen your burden and create an active, schoolwide interest in the play.

Students who are interested in directing can get experience by stage managing and watching you direct. The only way to learn directing is by doing it or watching others do it. If you are a beginner yourself, your stage manager can double as an assistant director. It is always good to have someone around with whom to discuss ideas and to share the pressure of rehearsals. By letting your stage manager have an active part in the production process, she will feel like she is contributing to the project and will give you invaluable assistance. Always remember that you need a very capable and reliable stage manager.

The point is to get a staff with whom you can share the burden, because, believe me, you will have a nervous breakdown if you try to organize, build, design, direct, and stage manage all by yourself. The bottom line is to get others involved. Your school should have plenty of students and teachers who are interested in helping you.

Costumes and Props, or Begging, Borrowing, and Stealing

Some great designs can be created from "found" materials from junkyards and thrift stores (and attics and basements). Never buy anything you can borrow or find used or thrown away. Again, the beauty of theatre is in its imagination and creating something from nothing (or at least very little). When I was directing *Ubu Roi*, the scene designer and I went to a junkyard and found old rusted pipes and machine parts which were incorporated into the set. An old office chair became a throne, a children's playground slide was used as a bridge. I once saw a children's play in which all of the costumes were made from garbage. Plastic bags, rugs, and old clothes were pieced together to create the costumes for an entire court of royal subjects. It is always cheaper and more effective to go this route, especially when money is scarce. Call around, explain that you're producing a play at the local school, and describe what you need. You'll be surprised to see what people have lying around. I once knew a scene designer who borrowed $1,000-worth of mirrored sheets of glass from a local store. (Just make sure you take care of anything you borrow and return it in as good a condition as you received it.) Anything is possible. I once made a "time machine" from a refrigerator box by poking holes in it and taking common household kitchen utensils (an egg beater, ice cube trays, a turkey baster) and attaching them to the box. Someone inside the box made the time machine look like it was alive with working parts by moving these objects and having them be animated on the outside. We even had "steam" coming from the machine by shooting baby powder through a hole in the top of the box. Recently, a designer with whom I worked created armor for a show with painted cardboard and papier-mâché, which was lighter and much less expensive than the real thing.

Solutions such as these are often very inexpensive and actually much more interesting and fun to create. Get together with your cast and brainstorm ideas for solutions to design and technical problems. Again, it is your imagination on which you need to rely, so don't think literally. Anything can be borrowed or found. A great place to find discarded materials is from the dumpsters of school art departments. Raiding garbage bins may not be glamorous, but it can be profitable. Besides, it is just going to get thrown away anyway. So, go for it!

Lighting and Sound

Lights and sound are much more complex than they seem. If anything goes wrong technically, it is usually one of these two things. I am not going to get into the fundamentals of lighting and sound here; they are far too involved. There are great books on lighting, including *The Magic of Light*, by Jean Rosenthal, and *Light on the Subject*, by Robert Hay. A wonderful book on sound design is *Sound for the Stage*, by Patrick M. Finelli. Read these books. They are invaluable. There are, however, some simple aspects of these designs that you should keep in mind.

LIGHTING

The very nature of light is intangible. It can't be held, folded, or fondled, but it certainly can be perceived and felt. Light is primarily an emotional statement. Just saying, "I'll use whatever's available" won't cut it. Usually, what's available is insufficient. More importantly, outdated electrical equipment could be potentially dangerous if it is not maintained properly.

If you are not familiar with lighting equipment and its usage, *simplicity* is always a good watchword. There are basically two kinds of lighting equipment that you'll encounter constantly: fresnels and lekos (a.k.a. ellipsoidals). Of course, there are many others, such as Par Cans and strip lights, but, basically, fresnels and lekos are the more commonly used.

Fresnels create "area" lighting. Because there is little control over the direction and "spill" of light, fresnels are used to "wash" an area of the stage (if not the entire stage) with light. Lekos are directional, and the beam of light can be shaped (with shutters) to provide more specific lighting effects and "specials" (lighting that defines a specific actor[s] or piece of scenery, singling it out from other people and objects on stage). A combination of the two is common, and if broken down in this way, can seem less complex and intimidating.

Lighting creates an emotional response in the audience. It works on a subliminal level that affects the psychology and emotional life of the audience member. For example, warmer colors (ambers, reds) can produce an energetic and vigorous feeling, whereas colder colors (blues) produce a harsher and less inviting response. Human beings respond in different ways to color and intensity of light. All people have subjective responses to visual and aural stimuli. As a director, you can respond only to what you sense is the appropriate atmosphere or mood. With lighting and sound, you create emotional responses that can be quite powerful and act on audience members in ways that you may not expect. The language of plays has a lyricism that you must get to know. A director can invite the audience into this lyrical world visually (through light) and aurally (through sound).

Lighting changes and cues respond to rhythmic and emotional changes that occur in the text, both on stage and on the page. Lighting cues are not solely about whether someone turns on a light switch when they enter a room, but can respond to changes in the emotional and psychological state of the characters. In my production of *Miss Jairus*, the characters were extremely influenced by superstitious fear and the hell-fire speeches of the local religious leader. As the vicar began his fire-and-brimstone speech, the lighting responded to the speech's intensity as it progressed and consumed the characters he was addressing. Like a fire that started small and began to burn out of control, the lighting environment followed this wildfire intensity, and the colors (reds and ambers) grew in intensity and saturation, creating the emotional heat and intensity the characters were feeling. There was no literal fire, nor did the setting change to correspond to this new environmental state, but it was true to the mood and emotions of the scene. It created a response in the audience based on the text and its performance and their physical and emotional responses to it.

SOUND

Sound is a very subjective design area indeed. Usually, it falls into the hands of the director, stage manager, or lighting designer/technician because it is not usually considered an imperative element of design. It is a very important part of the design process, however, and should not be overlooked.

As with lighting, sound is an intangible factor, perhaps even more so than lighting because it involves a sensory perception that we do not usually isolate, except, for example, when listening to music. People are influenced constantly by sound, and it affects us on a subliminal level. Close your eyes and listen to all of the sounds that surround you. Whether urban or rural, inside or outside, there is a constant level of white noise that is a mixture of all of the sounds created by machines and nature, combined into a single moment in time. The world hums along with a constant level of sound that subliminally affects each and every one of us daily.

There are two ways of creating sound for the stage: live and recorded.

Live Sound ■ Live sound is preferable to recorded sound because the audience, during the course of a performance, is accustomed to hearing and being in the same room with living and breathing actors. A recorded sound suddenly intrudes into the world of the play, and its nonliving quality jars with the live action. (If you have ever heard a tape recording of a telephone ringing on stage, you'll know what I mean.) Getting someone to create live sound backstage or on stage is also easier to cue and coordinate. Machines break down, and it is always easier to deal with people who can work with you and can anticipate any problems that may arise during the course of the performance. Because plays are live, their tempos and rhythms change every time they are performed. A person can adjust to these rhythms; a machine cannot. The machine remains inflexible and fixed in time and will not respond to the actor's changing rhythms.

Recorded Sound ■ The advantage of recorded sound is that, once it is recorded, you can simply push a button (if it works properly) and have what you want. Sound quality, however, is difficult to control, especially because most sound amplification equipment is not state of the art.

Whenever possible, I try to use live sound and performed music. You can rehearse with human beings and develop a working relationship that cannot be attained with a machine. For certain practical sounds, however, like an airplane or a car engine, recorded sound may be preferable, in accordance with the kind of equipment you may or may not have.

Technical Rehearsals

Technical rehearsals are important times for you and your stage manager. These are times of great stress, but if well managed, should run smoothly. There are two types of technical rehearsals: dry tech and "wet" tech.

DRY TECH

Give yourself the time to deal with technical problems. Have at least two technical rehearsals, one with actors and one without. The dry tech gives you a chance to run all the light and sound cues and any special effects without having the actors around.

You need to see if all the technical elements work properly, and this rehearsal also gives you time to fix anything that's not working. It doesn't waste your time, or the actors', due to sitting around waiting to see if something works. Go from one lighting or sound cue to the next without including the dialogue, just the cue lines, and test things out first so that your stage manager has a chance to go over all of the cues with the crew before the actors arrive.

"WET" TECH

A "wet" tech involves the actors and incorporates their cue lines so that they know technically what's happening around them. Do this before they get into costume so that they don't have too much to deal with all at once. Your stage manager will have the chance to coordinate her cues with the action on stage and the crew who are running the cues. This is a slow and tedious process, and everyone should be aware that it may last a long time, that they should stay calm, and they should understand that it may be tedious, but it is necessary.

There are ways to avoid potential technical disasters (*personal* ones can't be controlled, unfortunately). Make sure that the stage manager and actors check every prop, costume, and light before each and every show. Create a checklist of props and costumes. Do a "dimmer check," running through all of the light changes to ensure there are no burned-out lamps or electrical problems. Make sure all of your costumes and props are where they need to be. Lost or broken costumes and props are the causes of endless stress and chaos ten minutes before curtain. The smooth running of backstage is the stage manager's responsibility and is very important in keeping everyone sane and happy.

Survival of the Fittest, or "Letting Go of the Baby"

9

Well, you've made it. The show opened and no one was killed. But it's not over. There are still things to mind as the performances continue. Once you "let go of the baby" after opening night, you may think that your worries are over. Oh, no! As you sit in the audience and watch the nervous, first-time actors bumping into the furniture, forgetting lines and blocking; as you watch the prop gun click but not fire; as the door comes off of its hinges (and you come off of yours), you begin to wonder if it was all worth it. In fact, you have probably felt this way all through tech week. All of these things are beyond your control, and just like the parent watching his child stumble and fall, you must do the same. All you can do is provide emotional support and let whatever happens, happen. Hopefully, your stage manager is efficiency personified and reacts well during a crisis. This is all part and parcel of the theatrical experience. Live theatre means that the unforeseen will happen, and part of the live experience is seeing people at their imperfect best. Every show and every performance will be different. I have been directing for ten years, and every performance has its share of surprises. Just when everything is running smoothly, the lights go out or a costume tears or a prop gets lost (alas). The converse is also true, however.

Things will surprise you and go incredibly right, and moments that you never could have dreamed of will come to life before your very eyes. An actor creates an inspired moment, a sound cue that never quite clicked has now been perfected, suddenly that actor and costume have blossomed into a character of beauty and grace that you've never quite seen.

Each show has a life of its own. Each performance is unique from any other one before or after it. An unknown factor has entered into the equation. The party you have been waiting for has finally arrived: the audience. The audience is an essential element of the performance of any live event, whether it be theatre, music, or dance. A play is different from a film or museum exhibit in that the creation of the work is happening at the same moment it is being witnessed. The audience brings along its own energy and interests, and this changes the show's dynamics from performance to performance. You, in your role as director, have been the surrogate audience up until now, but once a group of people gather together to witness a performance, the quality of that performance is directly affected by the audience's presence. Each group of people brings unique responses and reactions to each show, and the members' interests are directly affected by what they see before them. Theatre is in, and of, the moment. It is not a creation of the past or a vision of the future, but a present reality that happens only when the audience and show come together. This is what makes theatre an exciting and unique artform.

The audience response is seemingly out of your control, but the fact that you've prepared, rehearsed, and brought the actors and crew along to this point is a testimony to the play's success and final result. Remember that process is just as important as product, and the director's work is in the process that has created this theatrical moment in time. It is the process of creating theatre that is your work, and your ultimate reward.

Theatre is ephemeral. The process and development of a play from page to actor to stage comes to an end with the striking of the set that follows closing night. One of the constant factors in the production of a play is that it does not last forever as a document (as in film); only the text of the play remains as a lasting testimony to the fact that the production ever took place.

So, why do we put all of this work into something that does not last? Are we merely masochists, masters of our own futility? Hardly. Theatre is about process. The journey of casting, rehearsal, tech, and performances cannot be attained through another process. The rehearsal process creates relationships, creative leaps, and discoveries that are presented to the live audience, and it is for this dynamic between audience and actor that theatre is created—that moment when the audience discovers what the actors have also discovered in the rehearsal process. The audience shares in this discovery because of its connection to the theatrical moment that is taking place right in front of its collective eyes. Once you remove the audience from this equation, the play is gone. That theatrical moment, however, lingers on in the hearts and minds of audience and actors alike, and nothing can replace that moment of recognition, that shared experience between people from all walks of life.

Your initial reading of the play, the first production meeting, the weeks of sharing ideas and dreams in rehearsal, the harrowing tech week, and the thrill of opening night will all come flooding back to you when closing night comes (all too soon), and the relationships you have developed with designers, stage manager, tech crew, publicity staff, school, and community will be what you and your actors take away as education, life experience, and lasting memories.

List of Play Publishers and Theatre Bookstores

Baker's Plays
100 Chauncy St.
Boston, MA 02111
(617)482-1280

Drama Book Shop
723 Seventh Ave.
New York, NY 10019
(212)944-0595

Dramatic Publishing Company
311 Washington St.
Woodstock, IL 60098
(815)338-7170

Dramatists Play Service
440 Park Avenue South
New York, NY 10016
(212)683-8960

Heinemann Educational Books
361 Hanover St.
Portsmouth, NH 03801-3959
(603)431-7894

I.E. Clark, Publisher
St. John's Road
Schulenburg, TX 78956–0246
(409)743–3232

Samuel French, Inc.
45 West 25th St.
New York, NY 10010
(212)206-8990

Samuel French's Theatre and Film Bookshop
7623 Sunset Blvd.
Hollywood, CA 90046
(213)876-0623